The Mechanical Triumphs of the Ancient Egyptians

This concise, erudite text will be of interest to any enthusiast of ancient Egypt or the mechanical arts. Among the topics included are the Egyptian knowledge of mechanics, the building of the pyramids, quarrying, the transportation of monuments and the erection of buildings and monuments.

T0347467

The Mechanical Triumphs of the Ancient Egyptians

Commander F.M. Barber

Routledge
Taylor & Francis Group

LONDON AND NEW YORK

First published in 2005 by
Kegan Paul International

This edition first published in 2010 by
Routledge
2 Park Square, Milton Park, Abingdon, Oxfordshire OX14 4RN

Simultaneously published in the USA and Canada
by Routledge
711 Third Avenue, New York, NY 10017

First issued in paperback 2014

Routledge is an imprint of the Taylor & Francis Group, an informa business

British Library Cataloguing in Publication Data
A catalogue record for this book is available from the British Library

ISBN 13: 978-0-7103-1004-0 (hbk)
ISBN 13: 978-0-415-65001-4 (pbk)

Publisher's Note
The publisher has gone to great lengths to ensure the quality of this reprint
but points out that some imperfections in the original copies may be
apparent. The publisher has made every effort to contact original copyright
holders and would welcome correspondence from those they have been
unable to trace.

INTRODUCTION.

As a result of three visits to Egypt it has been my experience that, notwithstanding the ultimate paramount interest of travellers in the manners and customs of the ancient Egyptians and the nature of their stupendous monuments, the question most frequently asked with regard to the latter is not why did they create them, but how. How did they transport these great stones, and how did they lift them to the positions in which they are now found ? In many cases the cause of this very practical inquiry is, perhaps, not far to seek, for this is a mechanical age, and it is probable that fifty per cent. of the people who visit Egypt to-day owe that privilege to the means derived from some application of the mechanic arts. With them the idea is instinctive ; but, indeed, with everybody it may be said that it is the physical problem which first attracts the mind, and not the æsthetic, or the ethnographic, or the religious.

It has been my object in preparing this essay to solve this problem in a more complete manner than has yet been done ; to show what is actually known and to suggest the most plausible theories, and thus to add my atom to the sum of human knowledge.

CONTENTS.

b

LIST OF ILLUSTRATIONS.

ILLUSTRATIONS IN TEXT.

FULL-PAGE ILLUSTRATIONS.

MECHANICAL TRIUMPHS OF THE ANCIENT EGYPTIANS.

CHAPTER I.

EGYPTIAN KNOWLEDGE OF MECHANICS.

ALL our knowledge of the ancient Egyptians goes to show that they were eminently a scientific and mechanical people. Thoth was the God of Science, and Tosorthros or Nebka, second king of the III. Dyn., B.C. 3766, was "skilled in the art of erecting solid masses of hewn stone" long before Cheops built the great pyramid, and the art never died out. Though there were civil wars and almost a blank in Egyptian history from B.C. 3133 to B.C. 2466, still when history does reappear, we find Usertesen I., B.C. 2433, erecting obelisks at Heliopolis, and each king thereafter for a thousand years surpassing his predecessor.

Moreover the ancient monarchs of all nations were for some unknown reason much given to erecting monolithic monuments of enormous size, and of using monstrous blocks in composite buildings. That it was considered a matter

B

of great merit is mentioned both in the Bible and in Josephus. This passion appears to have reached its maximum in Egypt, and the then known world, from the XVIII. Dyn., B.C. 1600, to the XX. Dyn., B.C. 1200. Whereas Cheops was content with stones weighing fifty to sixty tons in his pyramid, the two huge statues of Amenhotep III. (figs. xxi. and xxii.), wrought 2,300 years afterward, and even after 3,300 more years still sitting so solemnly in the great plain of Thebes, each weigh from 800 to 1,000 tons, and were only two of the many that formed the avenue leading to his mausoleum. A tablet found there dwells upon the magnificence of the temple and the size of the stone monuments he had erected in Thebes. " I have filled her with monuments in my name from the hill of the wonderful stones. Those who show them in their place are full of great joy at their size." Near by is the broken granite statue of Rameses the Great, weighing 900 tons, and at Tanis in lower Egypt, Prof. Petrie found the remains of another statue of Rameses of which the great toe was the size of a man's body, and the statue itself must have been 92 feet high and weighed more than 1,000 tons.

In Syria, at Baalbec, is a stone now lying in the quarry which weighs 1,100 tons, and measures 69 × 17 × 14 feet, and there are three more like it twenty feet up in the wall surrounding the Temple of the Sun a mile away. The date is approximately 1200 B.C. Solomon, who lived 1000 B.C., placed a ninety ton stone in the outer wall of Temple Hill at Jerusalem 100 feet above the ground, and the treasury of Atreus, near Mycenæ in Greece, built about the same time, has its portal covered with a stone weighing 130 tons. I do not speak of the marvels related by Herodotus, Diodorus, Mycrobius, Pliny and others. Those that I have mentioned can be seen to-day with the exception of the Tanis statue of Rameses, which was cut up to build a pylon by Orsoken II. about B.C. 900.

Ferguson, in his history of architecture, thinks that this handling of huge blocks was mere vanity; but it must be admitted that in a composite building it is a sound principle to have as few joints as possible, though modern architects, except shipbuilders, are disposed to ignore it, and in ancient times it was much more difficult to destroy a wall or a temple that contained huge blocks than it would be to-day. Even so late as the end of the sixteenth century, A.D., Hidyoshi placed stones in the castle wall at Osaka, Japan, which are 40 feet long and 10 feet thick, and no one knows how wide; they are probably wider than they are thick, but even if only 10 feet wide they would weigh 300 tons. It cannot be denied either that there is something more solemnly impressive about a huge stone statue than about anything that is merely joined together. The N. Y. Goddess of Liberty, 150 feet high, the sleeping Buddh of Bangkok, 160 feet long, are both beautiful and impressive; but in spite of their artistic merit every one knows that they are hollow, and that sense of beholding a stubborn triumph over nature is lost. They need care to prevent decay, and they will never remain of themselves an everlasting monument of the godlike power of a king. But for man himself nearly every monument erected in Egypt would be there to-day. Earthquakes and floods have done little, but Cambyses and his successors have done much. Two thousand statues were carried off to Babylon, two obelisks to Nineveh, two more to Constantinople and a dozen to Rome, while we moderns have our own samples of vandalism in Paris, London, and New York. Such statues of kings and gods as the ancients could not carry off they always tried to destroy, and it was to prevent this as much as possible that great size was deemed so important, and why the material so frequently chosen was granite, for the builder and the lime kiln were always the ready and deadly enemies of marble or other species of lime stone. Cheops suc-

ceeded in defying even these by the mere bulk
of his creation. When Abd-el-Lateef saw it at
the beginning of the thirteenth century A.D. it
was absolutely perfect, clad in all its glittering
casing, and although this has since gone to build
half the palaces of Cairo, it was but the peel of
the orange, the fruit itself has remained and
always will remain to astonish mankind.

This passion for gigantic undertakings and
the art of accomplishing them seems to have
been continued through the Greek Ptolemies to
the end of the Roman Empire. Though no
obelisks appear to have been cut after the
XVIII. Dyn., still they were continually being
moved about, and other objects, such as shrines,
sacrificial tables and sarcophagi, of even greater
bulk were quarried and transported throughout
the length of Egypt. In the quarries of Shellal
at the First Cataract can be seen two unfinished
statues of Amenhetop III., B.C. 1420, some un-
detached sarcophagi apparently intended for
sacred bulls of unknown date, and some smaller
detached sarcophagi or baths partly hollowed
out, and from their style undoubtedly of Roman
times, all within a stone's throw of each other.

Whatever methods were adopted by the
ancients they seem to have been continued on
down to the methods of the Romans without com-
ment on the part of any historian. During that

Empire, although art and taste degenerated, mechanical sciences still flourished; according to Professor Lanciani, the bronze statue of Nero, over 100 feet high, was moved in 121 A.D. by the architect Demetrianus from the site of the golden house of Nero in Rome to a spot near the Coliseum, a distance of 400 feet. "The displacement was effected with the help of twenty-four elephants, the statue remaining all the while upright and suspended from the movable scaffolding." There is now in the Colonna Gardens in Rome, a stone weighing twenty-seven tons, which formed part of the coping on top of the wall of the Temple of the Sun, which was built by Aurelian on the Quirinal Hill, A.D. 270. This stone was 150 feet above the Quirinal on one side, and 240 feet above the Campus Martius on the other side, which was a sheer precipice. Aurelian had visited Baalbec, and from graffitti found in the basement it is supposed that he employed Baalbec workmen. But the dark ages of Europe, from the fifth to the ninth century not only ceased all such undertakings, but they extinguished the knowledge of how they were accomplished. Of all the obelisks erected in Rome, the only one that remained standing was that of Caligula, which had been brought from Egypt in the first century A.D. and erected in his circus, and it is

astonishing to read that though various Popes
had wished for hundreds of years to remove it
to its present site in front of St. Peter's, no
engineer was found competent until in 1585,
when Pope Sextus V. succeeded after public
competition in securing the services of Fontana,
who successfully carried out the project in a
manner to be described later on.   Suffice it to
say at this point that he had unlimited command
of men and money, the right to clear away all
interfering buildings, and no one was allowed to
enter the inclosure under penalty of death.   Two
masses were held in St. Peter's to implore divine
assistance, and just before the operation commenced, the whole vast assembled multitude
knelt in prayer.   The pretty little anecdote about
the hardy sailor calling out at a critical juncture
to " wet the ropes," and thus saving the situation,
is told in connection with this enterprise, and
there is a family named Bresca in Bordighera
who have ever since retained the privilege of
supplying palm branches to St. Peter's on Palm
Sunday in consequence of it ; but the same story
is told about the cross on St. Isaac's, and about
the statue of Peter the Great in St. Petersburg,
and also about the raising of the obelisk in Paris,
and it seems hardly possible that there could be
truth in any of them.

How, then, were such gigantic undertakings

carried out by the ancient Egyptians who originated them? Obviously, from what has been
stated about there being no loss of continuity
from Cheops to Cæsar, the natural inference is
that approximately the same methods were always in use. These methods consisted in various
applications of the simple mechanical powers, *i.e.*,
the lever, the wheel and axle, the pulley, the inclined plane, the wedge and the screw. Besides
these the Romans knew of the power of torsion,
or twisted rope, of shrinkage from wetting and
of the elasticity of springs, and possibly of the
hydraulic press. They knew practically nothing
of steam, although its expansive power had been
discovered, or of electricity, though some of its
properties were understood. Their source of
power was always either men or animals, and it
should be noted here as a fact to be referred to
later on, that with such power the apparatus for
applying it always increases in complexity as the
amount of available power diminishes.

   To trace the origin, invention, or first use of
the simple mechanical powers is a most unsatisfactory undertaking. The arts of war have
found many historians, but the arts of peace
have had very few, and in Roman times it is
mostly by the study of the former that one arrives
at the latter. Vitruvius, the only ancient writer
on architecture whose works have come down

to us, lived in the time of Augustus, B.C. 28.
He was a most copious writer, but very obscure,
and all the drawings accompanying his ten books
having been lost, his translators and interpreters
have been obliged to construct plates from his
descriptions, often a difficult matter.

Of the machinery existing in his own day he
had an excellent practical knowledge, and his
knowledge of the methods of the ancients was
extensive : but unfortunately the word ancients
with him meant only the Greeks, who had a full
knowledge of all the mechanical powers, and he
never once mentions Egypt. It is only when
we come to study the Greeks themselves that
we are carried directly to Egypt, where, at
Heliopolis, the "On" of the Bible, was the
greatest university in the world. It had existed
from time immemorial under the domination
of the priests, whose number in the time of
Rameses III., B.C. 1225, amounted to thirteen
thousand. Here, more than two hundred years
earlier (Acts, vii. 22), Moses was instructed "in
all the wisdom of the Egyptians," which included,
according to Pollard, "arithmetic, geometry,
astronomy, medicine, music, and many other
subjects for which the university was famous."
Here were educated (600 B.C.) Solon, the law-
giver of Athens, and Thales of Miletus, the
discoverer of electricity. Manetho, the historian

of Egypt, was high priest here about 320 B.C., and in his time the library was the largest in the world ; it was transferred to Alexandria by Ptolemy Soter, B.C. 305, and from that day the university declined. Ptolemy, himself a Greek, encouraged the immigration which had commenced under Psamtik three hundred years before, and there arose that constant and familiar intercourse which led a celebrated writer to say that "the Egyptians originated, Greeks copied, seized on a beauty wherever they found it, and made it their own by improving it." Ptolemy invited Euclid to found the school of mathematics, and Archimides, born B.C. 287, came to this school when a young man. He was the greatest mathematician and the most inventive genius of antiquity ; to him are credited the discovery of the endless screw, the hollow screw in which water is drawn up and which he used for discharging the bilge water from the hold of a ship that Hiero, king of Syracuse, had built, and which he is also said to have used "in a journey made in Egypt to dry the lands inundated by the Nile." Pulleys and tackles, cog wheels and racks are also ascribed to him, and it was with a tackle and capstan that he surprised king Hiero by hauling a ship out of the water and up the beach. In his book vii., "On Bodies Floating in Liquids," he for the first time enunciates the principle of the hydraulic press or jack, *i.e.*, each particle of a fluid mass when in equilibrium is equally pressed in every direction. Larousse, in his "Grand Dictionnaire Universel," well says that "it is very likely that at this celebrated school of Alexandria he made himself acquainted with all anterior discoveries." Probably the same thing can be said of Hero, the discoverer of the steam engine, B.C. 130, and Ctesibus, the inventor of the force pump, B.C. 120.

Ptolemy Philadelphus, who succeeded Ptolemy Soter and was contemporary with Archimides, is described by Josephus and others as being very fond of the mechanical sciences : he erected the famous Pharos or lighthouse at Alexandria, 400 feet high ; he re-opened the canal between the Red Sea and the Nile, and he removed and re-erected obelisks. It is extremely probable that the fundamental principles of all the so-called inventions of Archimedes and other Greeks had already been discovered by the Egyptians ; but they had never been developed beyond a point adapted to their simple wants, as will be shown later.

That the Egyptians were acquainted with the principle of the lever is beyond a doubt. The weighing of the heart (fig. i.), as described in the Book of the Dead, a work already ancient in the time of Menes, the first recorded king, B.C. 4400, shows a lever of the first order, *i.e.*, where the fulcrum is between the power and the weight. A common shadoof (fig. ii.), which is conceded by all writers to be pre-historic in its origin, is another example. That the Egyptians had a knowledge of the wheel and axle is also plain. The sacred beetle with his ball of earth

FIG. I.   THE WEIGHING OF THE HEART.
Book of the Dead.

embodies sufficient idea of rotary motion in general, and Babylonian or cylinder seals, such as were found in the tomb of Menes, are an example of actual wheels. A vase of obsidian evidently turned in a lathe was found at the same time. Water wheels and the potter's wheel were always in use, and the employment of logs of wood for rollers hardly requires demonstration. A large wooden wheel was found

FIG. II. THE SHADOOF.

by M. Naville at Deir el Bahri in a tomb of the XI. Dyn., B.C. 2500, and in the museum at Cairo is a beautiful golden model of the bark of the dead, bearing a figure of Aahmes, B. C. 1600 : it is mounted on wheels three inches in diameter. Tomb paintings copied by Amelineau of the same date show the manufacture of chariot-wheels, and the tomb of Pahu, B.C. 1600, at El Kab shows a car on wheels. When we arrive at the Rameside dynasty two hundred years later, one sees innumerable sculptures of war chariots, and they were, according to Ebers, largely exported from Egypt at that time; but the most interesting specimen is the one now actually in the museum of Florence, which was found in a tomb at Thebes of the date of 1400 B.C. and is said to be Scythian and to have been captured in the north by some Egyptian warrior : but its wheels are exactly like those shown by Amelineau in process of manufacture in Egypt over two hundred years before. The lightness of this vehicle is something extraordinary, far exceeding that of an American trotting sulky : there is not a particle of metal about it, nothing but ash and leather, and yet this specimen must have been in actual use. Although it is under glass in the museum at Florence it is now being injured by worms.

The saqquieh (fig. iii.), is supposed by Wilkinson and most other writers to have been introduced into Egypt at the time of the Persian invasion, B.C. 527 : but Viollet le Duc, one of the most noted architects of the nineteenth century and the most painstaking historian of architecture, says, in his " Habitations of Man," that the saqquieh was common in Egypt in the first three dynasties. It is a most important point, for the saqquieh contains the principle of the capstan and the windlass.

That the ancient Egyptians had a knowledge of the pulley is a much debated point, most writers inclining to the opinion that they had not. There is a pulley supposed to have been for a well rope in the museum of Leyden, but its date is unknown ; and there is also a small wheel used as a reel for thread and inscribed with the name of a king of the XVIII. Dyn., B.C. 1600. In the museum at Cairo there are several specimens, a wooden cylinder 8 in. long by 5 in. diameter, with a hole for an axle and a small wooden block 3 in. by 2 in. with a wheel in one end, what sailors call a tail block, as there is a hole at the end opposite the wheel for a rope tail by which it can be made fast. There is also a stone wheel 10 in. in diameter and 3 in. thick, with a deep score in the circumference and a hole in the centre. They are all supposed

FIG. III.   THE SAQQUIEH.

to be ancient, but unfortunately no definite dates are known.

It is, however, not difficult to prove, in a manner I believe hitherto unattempted, that they not only had pulleys, but exactly how far they were advanced in the use of tackles for multiplying power. In Queen Hatasoo's " Expedition to Punt," about B.C. 1600, the boats represented on the walls of Deir el Bahri (figs. iv. and v.), must have been about 90 feet long, with one hoisting yard about 80 feet long and a square sail about 25 feet high. This yard made of pine or cedar would weigh at least 1,200 lbs., and the sail, made of No. 5 cotton canvas, suitable for boat sails, would weigh 300 lbs. The gear would weigh at least 300 lbs., making a total of 1,800 lbs. It will be observed that the crew of this boat consists of fifteen men on each side, besides a few sailors for going aloft, and it will also be seen that the halliards consist of two heavy single ropes each separately made fast to the yard by a clove hitch. These halliards lead up from the yard through a cage on top of the mast, then down aft and disappear below the rail of the boat ; undoubtedly, however, the end of each goes forward on its own side of the boat, passing by the men at the oars on that side so that they can haul on it when required without leaving their stations. Now the utmost power that a man can exert when pulling in that fashion is 100 lbs., and that only for a short time. Unless, then, there were large, well-greased pulleys both in the stern of the boat and in the cage at the masthead, the sail could not have been hoisted at all. Even with pulleys the loss by friction, according to the sailor's thumb rule, is one-sixth of the power exerted for every change of direction, and here there are two changes of direction, one at the stern and one at the masthead. The total power exerted by the men is 3,000 lbs., the loss by friction about 1,000 lbs., and the weight to be lifted 1,800 lbs. If instead of being hitched to the yard the halliards were hitched to the masthead and rove through a pulley on the yard and then back through a pulley at the masthead, it would have made the work of the crew one-half as great, but the time of hoisting the sail twice as long. Either the Egyptians did not know this or they did not care to save their men, for surely a royal fleet would have been supplied with the latest appliances of seamanship. Another proof of the knowledge of single pulleys is to be found in the lead of the numerous lifts which support the lower yards. They appear to pass through cheekblocks on the mast, and nearly the same thing is to be seen in a Burmese boat of the present day, though here the lifts

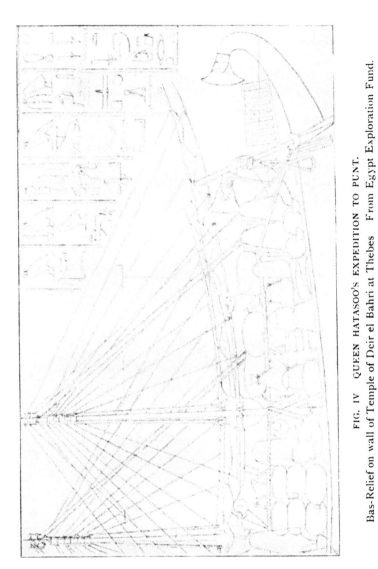

FIG. IV QUEEN HATASOO'S EXPEDITION TO PUNT.

Bas-Relief on wall of Temple of Deir el Bahri at Thebes From Egypt Exploration Fund.

are applied to the upper yard, because the sail
hauls out instead of hoists. The Burmese boat
presents a still older feature of Egyptian naval
architecture in the double mast, such as is seen
on the boat in the tomb of Ti in the V. Dyn., B.C.
3523. In Siam the Egyptian double steering
oar is still in use, and is hung to the boat in the
same way.

The inclined plane is of all the mechanical
powers the one rightly supposed to have been
most used by the ancient Egyptians. Herodotus
and Diodorus speak of it in connection with
the building of the pyramid of Cheops, and the
remains of two are to be seen at Gizeh. The
unfinished pylons of the great temple of Karnak
date from the Ptolemies, B.C. 300, and there are
the remains of inclined planes still against them
which may have been the original ones. Indeed, the Nile mud affords so convenient a
substance for constructing inclined planes of
sun-dried bricks that an engineer of the present
day would probably build a pylon at Thebes in
the same way, instead of using scaffolding and
cranes, provided that his human labour was unlimited in quantity. Lumber was always scarce
in Egypt ; the cedar, pine, and other light woods
were brought from Syria and were not of large
dimensions, as shown by the fished yards of
Queen Hatasoo's boats ; the acacia and syca-

more came from Ethiopia. Heavy timber was probably extremely expensive, and could only be afforded by royalty. The use of the wedge is but another application of the inclined plane, and was undoubtedly as well known to the ancient Egyptians as to ourselves.

The use of the screw is more difficult to trace than any other of the mechanical powers. We find among the tomb paintings excellent examples of the use of the brace and bit and the whip drill for boring holes; but it does not follow that the bit was of the shape of a screw, for a spoon drill might have been used. Certainly no large screws have been found; but as it is the simplest instrument for converting a motion of rotation into a motion of translation, it is strange if such a mechanical people did not know of it. They were excellent rope makers, and this manufacture itself might almost have suggested it. Vitruvius speaks of screw oil presses being in use by the Greeks and Romans, and the Egyptians were large consumers of olive oil.

They were also acquainted with the effects of torsion or twisting, as shown in some of the tomb paintings of wine making, and in Queen Hatasoo's boats (figs. iv. and v.) can be seen many rope loops with sticks thrust in them and twisted opposite ways; as fine examples of a

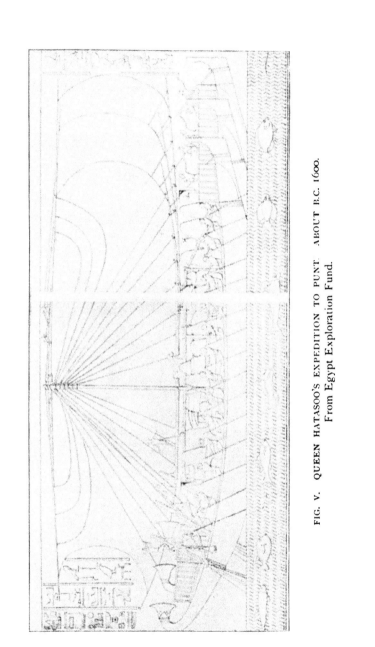

FIG. V. QUEEN HATASOO'S EXPEDITION TO PUNT. ABOUT B.C. 1600.
From Egypt Exploration Fund.

" Spanish windlass" as any seaman of to-day could make, and it might be added that there are many other wrinkles of seamanship shown in these boats, such as grommets, half hitches, round turns, furling lines, selvagees, etc., which give an added meaning to the time-worn saying that there is nothing new under the sun, and in the 99th chapter of the ritual translated by Wilkinson from Lepsius, the halliards are called " S'et tut," which bears a strange resemblance to our term " set taut," the order given preliminary to hoisting a sail.

Regarding the Egyptian knowledge of hy-draulics and hydrostatics, we can only infer that it was extensive enough to meet their requirements. They were a nation of sailors and agriculturists, and as the life of the nation depended upon the Nile, such problems must have been continually presented to them.   One can see to-day the water screw used in the lower Nile, where the banks are low, and also the tâbût, a kind of wheel with hollow felloes, the shadoof where the banks are higher, and the saqquieh where they are still higher, and in the Fayum great automatic undershot waterwheels, 30 feet in diameter, with pottery buckets, which Mr. John Ward in his in-teresting "Pyramids and Progress," says are deemed by Major Brown, R.E., Director-General of Irrigation, so much more economical for the purpose than any modern substitute, that they are being repaired instead of replaced. The same wheels are found in China. Inasmuch as all writers agree that the maximum of Egyptian civilization was found in the time of Menes, where history commences, it certainly seems plausible, as M. With says in his history of the mechanical powers, that Archimedes found the water screw already in existence. We have tomb pictures of the siphon and bellows with valves 1,500 B.C., and in Ctesibus' day there were valves in the buckets of "improved" saq-quiehs; possibly the force pump idea came from there, as others have suggested.

Mechanically speaking the Greeks discovered the Egyptians just as the Jesuits discovered the Chinese three hundred years ago. In both cases there was found the same rudimentary know-ledge of all the sciences, arts, and professions, but the development of none, and in both cases there was the same cause, *i.e.*, the density of the population. In China, as Williams says, "there are a million people for every day of the year," and they are all crowded to the coasts and river valleys. In ancient Egypt there were 8,000,000 people crowded into a space of only 11,500 square miles, thus giving a density of 695 per square mile. Belgium, the most populous country in Europe and the nearest to ancient

Egypt in size, has 6,410,700 in a space of 11,370 square miles, giving a density of 563 per square mile. According to both Buckle and Malthus, there was never such a country as ancient Egypt for producing population. There were unlimited dates and durrah for food, and the climate, by its heat, both diminished the appetite and rendered clothing unnecessary. According to Diodorus, who visited Egypt about 50 B.C., it did not cost more than twenty drachmas—about three dollars and a quarter—to bring up a child to manhood. There were few foreign wars in ancient days, and beyond an occasional famine there was nothing whatever to check the increase of population. The result of such a situation, so far as concerns the mechanical sciences, is invariably to stifle them altogether or to divert them from their original purpose of economizing human labour into a means for employing it. China boasts a civilization as old as that of Egypt, and yet the Chinese never advanced beyond the single pulley any more than was apparently the case with the Egyptians. They had also a rude windlass, because there are some situations where human power takes up too much space if attached to a rope; probably the Egyptions had the same. Now the Chinese are an extremely ingenious and inventive people, and have many other traits in common with the ancient Egyptians, including a dislike of foreigners, for the Greeks were bitterly detested for ages after they were allowed to enter Egypt, and were for centuries confined, as a trading community, to Naukratis. Patient and persevering to the last degree, the Chinese have a genius for simplicity in mechanical devices which enables them to produce results requiring much more complicated appliances in other countries. It has never been the ambition of the rulers of China to create gigantic personal monuments, as was the case in Egypt ; but in whatever they have attempted they have succeeded. The Great Wall was built by Tsin-chi-Hwangti ; it was finished B.C. 204, having been ten years in building. It was 1,500 miles long, and, according to Williams, would stretch from Philadelphia to Topeka, or from Portugal to Naples. In its main portion it is 30 to 40 feet high and 25 feet thick, built of many thicknesses of brick, with towers at intervals, and filled in with rubble. The bricks are $15\frac{1}{4} \times 7\frac{1}{4} \times 3\frac{1}{2}$ inches, and weigh about 60 lbs. each. Nearly the whole of the wall passes through a mountainous country, one peak which it surmounts being over 5,000 feet high, and at Shan-hai-quan, where it comes down to the sea, the heights are so precipitous, that the legends of the natives assert that the bricks were carried

up one at a time on the backs of goats. All
writers, except Pumpelley, speak of this wall as
a military absurdity and a monument of labori-
ous folly; but its object was to keep out the
Tartars, and I was struck, when I was there,
with the fact that even to this day the natives
outside the wall at Shan-hai-quan go well armed
while those inside the wall carry no arms whatever. The Grand Canal and the old high road
from Pekin to Canton, over 1,200 miles long,
are other examples of enormous expenditure of
human labour, and Polam bridge on the old
high road, about forty miles from Amoy, is
truly Egyptian in the simplicity and massive-
ness of its conception. Several of the stones
of which it is composed measure 78 feet long
by 5 feet square, and weigh 140 tons each.
They must have been gotten into position by
the simple mechanical appliances which we
know the Chinese to have possessed, aided
probably by the tide. At the great hall of
the Ming tombs, near Pekin, the roof is supported by 32 columns of teak, each one 32
feet long and over 12 feet in circumference.
They weigh 15 tons each, and must have been
brought over 2,000 miles by sea and 30 by
land, or possibly all the way by land, for Siam
is the nearest teak-growing country. Other examples might be cited, and it can also be said

that even to-day Chinese engineers will stop a breach in the bank of a flooding river that would defy any engineer in Europe. Huge fascines made of millet stalks, bamboo ropes, boats, baskets, and myriads of workmen, properly directed, constitute the entire equipment. It was these myriads of workmen, properly directed, that enabled the ancient Egyptians to accomplish their great works with the simplest of mechanical appliances. The government was a despotism, where the rich were very rich and the poor very poor, and the labour market was flooded. This threw all the labour of the country into the hands of the few, who had education enough to guide it, and whatever may be said of the grinding misery of the people under the early Pharaohs, it was probably necessary to keep them fed and employed, either to prevent starvation or idleness, which is sure to breed mutiny, as every ship captain knows, and Pliny says the Egyptians were lazy. When the Nile was in flood there must have been a vast unemployed population, and Professor Petrie thinks that it was at this season only that the work on the pyramids was performed. The question of misery also is relative, and depends upon the point of view. We look upon every man as a reasoning being with a soul, but in the Orient a coolie has no soul, and his life

is only more valuable than that of a dog, because a dog can be eaten after he is dead and
a coolie cannot.   Such people have every appearance of being merely talking animals, and
their only conversation is of rice and cash, with
absolutely no variation whatever.   According
to Miss Fielde, not one man in a hundred in
China can read, and of women not one in a
thousand.   Xerxes had 2,000,000 men and
3,000,000 camp followers in his army when he
invaded Greece B.C. 480, but they were con-
trolled almost entirely by the whip, and in order
to number them it was necessary to drive them
through a walled inclosure holding exactly
10,000.   The standard of intelligence and education could not have been very different in ancient
Egypt.   Herodotus says that there were 20,000
cities, and Diodorus says 18,000.   The refuse
population here must have been enormous, judging from Oriental counterparts.   Public works
were a necessity, and apparently they took the
form of tombs and monuments, and judging
from the texts and the paintings dealing with
the subject of forced labour, a large portion
of the duty of the standing army of 400,000
men must have been that of guards.   Both the
army and the labouring classes were thus kept
fully occupied.

CHAPTER II.

ACCORDING to Maspero the construction of pyramids was a common state affair from the beginning of the IV. Dyn., B.C. 3733, to the end of the XIV. Dyn., about B.C. 2200, and of the sixty or seventy which still exist, the three at Gizeh are the most notable. They are situated seven miles from Old Cairo upon a rocky plateau about 100 feet high (figs. vi. and vii.) at the edge of the Great Sahara Desert and overlooking the valley of the Nile, and they all contain various passages and chambers that are connected with the outside by a tunnel, the mouth of which was closed by a stone undistinguishable from the rest of the surface. The investigations of Professor Petrie, the latest authority on pyramids, 1880, seem to show that the closing stone worked on a horizontal hinge of stone, so that the tunnel was at all times accessible to the priests. The principal pyramid at Gizeh is that of Cheops, B.C. 3733. It is located about one thousand feet from the edge of the plateau, and, according to Professor Petrie, it was opened

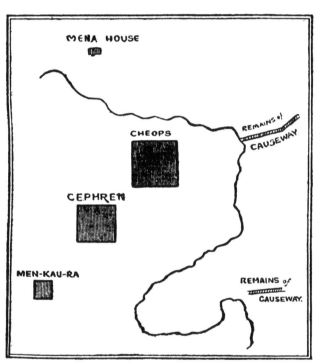

FIG. VI.

during the civil wars from B.C. 3100 to B.C. 2500;
it was again opened by the Persians between
500 and 600 B.C., and probably also by the
Romans. All of these people seem to have
known of the entrance, for no writer makes any
mention of its being concealed : but at the time
of the Khalif Mamoun, A.D. 813 to 833, this
knowledge had disappeared, and he quarried a
tunnel into the middle of the north side a few
feet above the ground. After penetrating some
100 feet his engineers cut into the original
tunnel, whose mouth being traced back was
found to be 23 feet on one side of the spot the
Khalif had naturally selected for tunnelling.
Since that time the entrance has never been
closed. This pyramid is considered by every
authority to be the greatest monument in the
world, and the fact that it is also the oldest
monument, excepting possibly the step pyramid at Saqquara, lends an additional interest to
any investigation as to the methods by which
it was constructed. It is difficult in the first
place for the mind to grasp the amount of
human labour that is concentrated in this one
spot, and perhaps an abundance of detail may
assist in this respect. We know from Professor
Petrie that it is nearly 756 feet square and 451
feet high, and that originally it was 481 feet high.
It is composed of 206 courses of lime stone

FIG. VII.   THE PYRAMIDS AT GIZEH, SHOWING HEIGHT OF PLATEAU.

that vary irregularly from 4 feet 10 inches to 2 feet 2 inches in height, and the blocks of stone in the mass vary in weight from two to sixty tons, the largest being the ones that cover the king's chamber. The entire pyramid was originally covered with a smooth stone casing such as can still be seen at the top of the second pyramid. Several blocks of it remain in place at the base, and they weigh about sixteen tons each. The pyramid covered thirteen and a half acres of ground, which is more than six London blocks and more than the whole of Lincoln's Inn Fields, and contained eighty-nine million cubic feet of stone, which if drawn out in a line a foot square would reach two-thirds round the earth. It is nearly three times as large as St. Peter's at Rome, and fifty feet higher; but, as Miss Edwards says, there is nothing which gives one so impressive an idea of its size as to watch its mighty shadow creeping across the Nile valley when the sun is setting behind it. Buckle, in his "History of Civilization" says that Herodotus in 450 B.C., and Diodorus in 50 B.C. were the only two ancient historians who actually visited Egypt: the former obtaining his information from the priests at Heliopolis and the latter from the priests at Thebes. Buckle thinks Herodotus the most accurate. According to him, 100,000 men were employed for twenty years in building the pyramid of Cheops, and according to Diodorus, 366,000 men were employed for the same length of time. Taking Herodotus' figures, and assuming that they did no night work, the actual working time becomes ten years of continuous, unremitting labour, and calculating according to Haswell's tables, five men to one-horse power, we have a force of 20,000 horse power, which would be sufficient to drive a 10,000 ton steamer at the rate of 20 knots per hour seventy times round the world in that time. Supposing, lastly, that the pyramid could be made to slide on its base, it would require 101,000,000 men to drag it along.

Maspero well says of this pyramid, "We may touch hundreds of courses of blocks, 200 cubic feet in size, and thousands of others scarcely less in bulk, and we are at a loss to know what force has moved, transported and raised so great a number of colossal stones . . . what machinery they had, and in proportion to our inability to answer these questions we increasingly admire the power which regarded such obstacles as trifles." And Ferguson in his history of Architecture thus sums up: "No one can possibly examine the interior of the Great Pyramid without being struck with astonishment at the wonderful mechanical skill displayed in its construction. The immense blocks of granite brought from Syene, a distance of 500 miles, polished like glass, and so fitted that the joints can scarcely be detected! Nothing can be more wonderful than the extraordinary amount of knowledge displayed in the construction of the discharging chambers over the roof of the principal apartment, in the alignment of the sloping galleries, in the provision of the ventilating shafts, and in all the wonderful contrivances of the structure. All these, too, carried out with such precision that, notwithstanding the immense superincumbent weight, no settlement in any part can be detected to an appreciable fraction of an inch. Nothing more perfect mechanically has ever been erected since that time." And Rawlinson concludes as follows: " The architectural effect of the two greatest pyramids is certainly magnificent. They do not greatly impress the beholder at first sight, for a pyramid, by the very law of its formation, never looks as large as it is, it slopes away from the eye in every direction, and eludes rather than courts observation. But as the spectator gazes, as he prolongs his examination and inspection, the pyramids gain upon him, their impressiveness increases. By the vastness of their mass, by the impression of solidity and durability which they produce, partly also, perhaps, by the symmetry and harmony of their lines and their perfect simplicity and freedom from ornament, they convey to the beholder a sense of grandeur and majesty, they produce within him a feeling of astonishment and awe, such as is scarcely caused by any other of the erections of man."

The full object of the construction of the pyramid of Cheops will never be known. After years of discussion of this curious topic, the scientific world has reached the conclusion that pyramids were tombs and nothing but tombs : at the same time, however, the extraordinary mathematical properties of this one (whatever we may think of their peculiar application by Piazzi Smyth, Menzies, and others in order to demonstrate the obscurities of the Bible) certainly impresses one with the idea that this pyramid at least was more than a tomb. The fact that it is in latitude $30°$, that it faces exactly the true north, and its entrance tunnel points to the North Pole ; that its angle of $52°$ causes it to become an exact integral part of the solid contents of the earth : that it expresses the relation between the diameter and circumference of a circle, the relation between the side and hypotenuse of a right triangle, the distance of the earth from the sun, the nature of the orbit of the earth round the sun, and the proportion of that revolution to that of the earth

round its own axis, the length of that axis, etc.,
etc.   Surely all these cannot be the purely acci-
dental accompaniments of the tomb of a tyrant.
When one considers, too, the inexplicable and
yet exact arrangement of the various chambers
and galleries, and that there is room for 3,700
more such chambers, provided we could find
them, we can almost be tempted to believe that
we have not yet discovered all the chambers or
even the true chamber of Cheops, for Herodotus
says that before the pyramid was built a channel
was cut from the Nile and an island made underneath the foundation, and that this island contains the tomb of the king.   This chamber must
be at least 50 feet underneath the lowest chamber
yet discovered, and not necessarily directly below
that one, as Colonel Vyse seemed to have thought
when he sunk a pit there.   It might lie under
any part of the structure, for investigation in
all pyramids has demonstrated the fact that
the original architects expended a vast amount
of ingenuity in creating false chambers and
passages, for no other purpose apparently than
to deceive and delay as long as possible the
future rifler of the tomb.

In the construction of the Great Pyramid the
highest type of the mason's art is shown.   The
bulk of the stones are squared and rough
finished, and united by a mortar apparently

composed of sand, lime and crushed red pottery, as it has a slightly pinkish color ; but the granite slabs which line the chambers and galleries are united with the utmost nicety without cement. The exterior coating exhibited the same exquisite accuracy, and Abd-el-Lateef, thirteenth century, A.D., says that the blocks were adjusted with a nicety so precise that "not even a hair or a needle can be inserted between any two of them." Professor Petrie confirms this statement, and says in addition that the joints which he found between the casing blocks remaining at the foot of the pyramid were not only almost invisible but "they were cemented." Herodotus tells a curious story about the outside of the pyramid, showing an inscription stating the amount of money that was expended, £200,000, in radishes, onions and garlic for the workmen. These so-called inscriptions may have been of a religious character or merely graffiti, the scrawlings of workmen and travellers, such as are to be found on all the other monuments of Egypt. There is little doubt, however, that something was there, for Professor Budge states that "William of Baldensel, who lived in the fourteenth century, tells us that the outer coating of the two largest pyramids was covered with a great many inscriptions arranged in lines." Possibly, as Miss Edwards suggests, when the future archæologist shall investigate the ruins of Cairo, he will find many of the stones of the palaces to have pyramid hieroglyphics on the inside surface, and these may then be translated.

The limestone of the pyramid came partly from the plateau upon which it is located and partly from the quarries of Masara and Tûra in the Mokattam hills on the opposite side of the Nile and about twelve miles distant in a south-east direction.   The two quarries are very near together and in ancient times the rock must have had a perpendicular face; this being cut away, tunnels were run into the hills and the rock worked out from there.   The remains of an inclined plane can still be seen leading to the river less than half a mile away, and the deep scores in the road show where the runners of the sledges have passed.   These sledges, or similar ones, which are to be seen in the Gizeh museum, show the crudest form of workmanship; but it was ample for the purpose intended.   In one of the quarries at Masara is a representation of a block of stone drawn by six oxen (fig. viii.), with an inscription showing that this was one of the methods employed in the time of Aahmes I. XVIII. Dyn., B.C. 1600.   Professor Petrie found the same picture among the broken stone of Illahun pyramid of the time of the XII. Dyn., B.C. 2466.   This shows a continuity of practice of 800 years which is quite Chinese in its character. From this Masara picture many writers have inferred that this was the method adopted by the pyramid builder 3,000 years before. It may have been one of the methods, but in that day of teeming population it was probably too expensive to have been the usual one. The block shown on this ox sledge is apparently a huge one being 8 feet long and 4 feet high : but it must be a very thin one or six oxen could not draw it. A 600 lb. ox can only exert a force of

FIG. VIII.   STONE ON OX SLEDGE.

150 lbs. at the rate of a mile and a half an hour for eight hours, or 900 lbs. for the six oxen. The weight that can be thus pulled under ordinary circumstances is about five times the tractive power, as will be shown later, and this limits the block to a weight of 4,500 lbs. Estimating Egyptian limestone to weigh 166 lbs. per cubic foot, we find that the block can only be 10 inches thick. It is standing on its edge, and judging from the width of the sledges in the Gizeh museum this must have been usually the case. The stones on top of the pyramid

average roughly 4 × 3 × 2 feet, they would weigh about four-fifths as much as this one, and probably there are few others in the pyramid so small.   Man power would be cheaper than oxen for a twenty years' contract in hauling such stones.   Why, said an old mandarin to a missionary in the interior of China, should we employ an ox (water buffalo) when five men can live on the same amount of food ? the ox can only work in one place while the men can work in five, and he cannot live nearly so long as a man.   When draught animals and men live on the same food, as is the case in China and was the case in Ancient Egypt, the problem of the relative value of man power and animal power is reduced to its simplest equation.

Between the pyramid and the Nile was another inclined plane whose remains can yet be seen (fig. vi.)   It is thus described by Herodotus : "The time during which the people were thus harassed by toil lasted ten years on the road which they constructed, along which they drew the stones, a work in my opinion not much less than the pyramid, for its length is five stades—about 3,000 feet,—and its width ten orgyæ—60 feet, and its height, where it is the highest, eight orgyæ —48 feet, and it is of polished stone with figures carved on it."   It is evident that Cheops' engineer thoroughly understood the advantages of a good road bed in its relation to facility of transport, a matter of extreme importance, for one thing which causes the works of the ancient Egyptians to appear so incredible, is that we now see them all over Egypt surrounded by mountains of sand or seas of mud, with scarcely a vestige of a road anywhere. From an inquiry made by the U.S. Dept. of Agriculture in 1895, the fact was developed that in the U.S. the cost of transport of one ton of farm produce over wagon roads, was 25 cents per mile, while the average cost in Europe was 8·6 cents, the difference being mainly due to the quality of the roads, the European farmer being able to haul three or four tons at a load, while U.S. farmers were only able to haul a ton or less than a ton. With a solid stone road bed such as the Egyptians had, they would not have wasted their man power, and there is an additional advantage in a solid stone road bed where sleds are used in the fact that grease, liberally applied, diminishes the traction very much by reducing the friction. Fig. xvi., which will be discussed later on, represents the only picture that has come down to us from the ancient Egyptians themselves as showing their method of transport of a colossus. A man can be seen there pouring oil on the road bed. In many other tomb pictures also, one sees life-sized statues of the deceased being drawn on sleds.

In all cases there is a man pouring oil in front of the runners. The process is familiar to everyone who has seen a ship hauled out of the water or launched into it, and twenty-five years ago at Madeira there were nothing but ox sleds for hauling both goods and passengers over the cobble stone pavement, the driver walking beside with a piece of pork rind attached to his whip lash, and which he adroitly flicked under the runners from time to time.

Herodotus says that the plateau upon which Cheop's pyramid stands (fig. vii.) is "about one hundred (Greek) feet high," 104 English feet, and if the calculations of Wilkinson and Lane are correct, and the Nile valley in this portion of it rises at the rate of about 4 to 5 inches per 100 years, then at the time of Cheops, the plateau must have been about 120 feet high. If now we make a scale-drawing (fig. ix.) of the pyramid, the plateau and the Herodotus incline, we find that the height of the latter, 8 orgyæ, or 48 feet, is less than half what it ought to be. As Herodotus saw this incline and must have measured it himself, as he says he measured the pyramids, and moreover as it must have been in his day the public high road, it is reasonable to suppose that 18 orgyæ are meant instead of 8 orgyæ: this would give a height of 108 feet, which is reasonably near the height of 104 feet which he gives for the plateau.   If the plateau had been cut through at the height of 8 orgyæ, and the incline continued to the pyramid site 1,000 feet distant, such a cutting would have remained to this day, but there is none there. M. Amélineau says that the remains of an inclined plane leading to the second pyramid still existed at the end of the eighteenth century, and the ruins of the one leading to the third pyramid are still visible (fig. vi.).   It illustrates the prodigality of human labour in that day to think that all three pyramids must have been built within 100 years, and that each had its own inclined causeway for transporting the material.   With an inclined plane 3,000 feet long, and 120 feet high, the incline would only have been 1 foot in 25, a very easy grade indeed on a greased stone causeway, and the next point is to show how much human power was necessary to haul stones over it.

Various experiments have been made in different countries in regard to man power, and it is found that he can exert a force varying all the way from 150 lbs. down to nothing according to the position which he is compelled to assume. Harnessed in traces like a horse, he can exert for a few moments a force of 75 to possibly 100 lbs., but he cannot keep it up, and the moment he commences to move the rate falls rapidly.

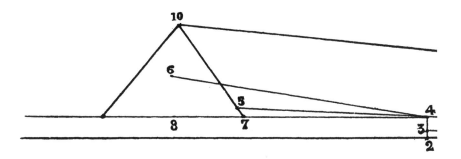

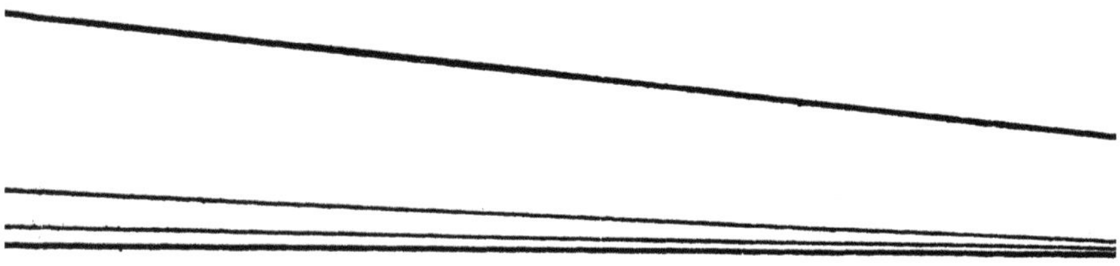

FIG. IX.

ne.

    as it must have been.

       „   „   prolonged to Pyramid entrance.

where heaviest stones are found.

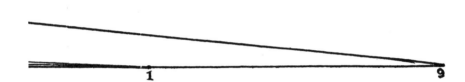

SCALE, 500 ft. to 1 in.

According to Maschet's tables, for steady pulling at the rate of $1\frac{1}{2}$ mile per hour for 8 hours per day, it falls as low as 30 lbs. Though the Egyptians were a light built people they worked under the lash like ordinary cattle, and at least this amount of force must have been obtained from each man, though probably not more, for it must have been to the interest of their task masters to have worked them regularly each day and to have kept them in fair physical condition. Thirty pounds per man therefore is a reasonable estimate. For the amount of power necessary to drag a body on a cradle along greased ways, it was found by M. Le Bas the eminent French Naval Constructor who brought the Paris obelisk from Luxor in 1832, that an estimate of $\frac{1}{5}$ to $\frac{1}{6}$ of the total weight of the object was ample for all grades up to 1 foot in 10. We can assume then that $\frac{1}{5}$ is a fair proportion. Applying these conditions to the heaviest stone in the pyramid, 60 tons, and we have a force of 12 tons actually to be applied to drag it to the pyramid plateau, a force represented by about 900 men. Harnessed in double rank on four draft ropes, they would cover a space on the causeway about 225 feet long by 16 wide, a very manageable and compact force, the stone itself being about $27 \times 6 \times 4\frac{1}{2}$ feet, and as Herodotus' road was 60 feet wide, there was ample room for three such bodies at one time.

As will be seen later the Egyptians in the time of Hatasoo, B.C. 1600, were capable of building barges or lighters for transporting two obelisks at one time, even if placed end to end. Such lighters must have been at least 250 feet long. Probably in Cheop's time they could do the same, for civilization ran backward in Egypt, and if such were used for the ferry across the Nile, about 6 miles, the force of 900 men could have marched directly on board with their stone and off again without the necessity of any lifting machines for moving the stone from the land to the boat and *vice versa*.   As the ferry was down stream, the entire trip from the quarry to the pyramid could have been made in one day.

The granite blocks in the pyramid were brought from Assouan at the First Cataract. They are quarried there from boulders or from the face of the rock about a mile from the right bank of the Nile and only a few feet above it. I have never seen in Egypt any ancient pit quarries where machinery would have to be used to hoist out the blocks.   The transportation of these stones was effected by means of lighters or rafts.   Most writers incline to the latter idea : but the Egyptians appear from tomb paintings to have been capable of constructing any kind of floats from dug-out canoes to built-up ships, and it is doubtful if rafts pure and simple have sufficient buoyancy for the purpose. In the VI. Dyn., B.C. 3233, Una, an engineer of Pepi I., was sent to the quarries of Hatinubu for an alabaster table of offerings. According to Wilkinson, he transported the huge stone to Saqquara on a raft 60 × 30 cubits, which be built in seventeen days. The time here shows that it could not have been a lighter; but the royal cubit being equal to 20·7 inches, this raft would have measured 104 × 52 feet, and if made of 12 inch locust logs, the common ship-building timber of Egypt, would have had a carrying capacity of only 27 tons. It must, therefore, have been supported by boats to give it greater buoyancy, or in other words it was a floating bridge or pontoon. It might also have gained additional buoyancy from inverted earthenware vessels such as were common twenty years ago in Egypt, where they were brought to market at Alexandria in this manner. Rafts of this kind are common on the Ganges in India and Yangtse in China, on the latter river the earthenware vessels are as large as hogsheads. On the coast of Brazil north of Pernambuco all the navigation between ship and shore is performed by means of rafts made of Jaugada wood, which is almost as light as cork, yet very few tons of dead weight can be carried. On the north coast of Celebes in the Dutch East Indies, ebony is brought off on huge rafts of light wood, but few blocks can be carried at once, and the rafts are under water nearly all the time.   Stone represents such a concentrated weight, that lighters must have been more in use by the ancient Egyptians than rafts.

CHAPTER III.

HAVING discussed the methods by which the stones were brought to the pyramid plateau we finally come to the vexed problem of how they were placed in position. Every writer on the subject of Egypt has had something to say with regard to it; but among ancient writers the accounts are simply variations of what was written by Herodotus and Diodorus. They were the only ones who received their opinions at first hand from the Egyptian priests, the sole source of scientific knowledge until their religion was abolished in A.D. 379; and their statements are therefore worth repeating. Cary's literal translation of Herodotus from the text of Baehr is as follows: "This pyramid was built thus: in the form of steps which some call crossae, others bomides. When they had first built it in this manner, they raised the remaining stones by machines made of short pieces of wood: having lifted them from the ground to the first range of steps, when the stone arrived there, it was put on another machine that stood

ready on the first range : and from this it was
drawn to the second range on another machine :
for the machines were equal in number to the
ranges of steps : or they removed the machine,
which was only one, and portable, to each range
in succession, whenever they wished to raise
the stone higher : for I should relate it in both
ways, as it is related.   The highest parts of it,
therefore, were first finished and afterwards
they completed the parts next following : but
last of all they finished the parts on the ground,
and that were lowest."   Diodorus says : " The
stone is said to have been brought from Arabia
(the east side of the Nile was in ancient days
called the Arabian shore) a considerable distance and the building made by means of
mounds (inclined planes) machines not having
yet been invented."   He then goes on to
wonder what had become of these mounds.
The Egyptians told him that they were composed of nitre and salt and dissolved by water
when no longer required : but Diodorus does not
believe this, and concludes that " The same
number of hands that raised the mounds removed the whole to the original place whence
they were brought." Wilkinson, who has written
the most comprehensive existing work on the
manners and customs of the ancient Egyptians,
1831, and Colonel Howard Vyse, who, in 1837,

made the first accurate modern survey of the pyramids, are both of the opinion that the machine of Herodotus for raising the blocks was similar to the "Polyspaston" described by Vitruvius. Polyspaston, or many pulleys, is, according to Newton's translation, the term applied by Vitruvius to a species of two-legged sheers supporting tackles. Newton supplies an illustration drawn from Vitruvius's description, which is accurate in principle; but fig. x. is the exact representation, since it is from a sculpture on a tomb [probably that of an architect] of the early Roman Empire, B.C. 44 to 29, and now in the Lateran Museum in Rome. So far as I am aware it is the oldest contemporary illustration of a combination of tackles in existence. In support of his view Colonel Vyse says : " In blocks of each course where visible, are holes 8 inches in diameter and 4 inches deep, apparently to support the machinery described by Herodotus." I have never been able to find such holes ; but I have never had his opportunities for making a thorough search. He also says : " In front of the northern face of Cheops are several rows of 4 or 5 feet apart of three or four circular holes in the level rock about 12 inches in diameter, and 8 to 10 inches deep, probably to support sheers or scaffolding for turning the blocks."

Such holes are, of course, usually covered with sand. Professor Petrie (1881) has another theory as follows : " It would be very feasible to employ the method of resting them (the stones) on two piles of wooden slabs, and rocking them up alternately to one side and the other by a spar under the block, thus heightening the piles alternately, and so raising the stone. This would also agree with the mysterious description of a machine made of short pieces of wood (Herodotus), a description of which it is otherwise difficult to realize." Murray's "Handbook of Egypt" speaks of this mode of constructtion as being "the most probable." In my opinion the methods described by Herodotus and Diodorus are sufficient to account for the building of the main portion of the entire pyramid, except the casing, without resorting to so complicated a machine as that of Colonel Vyse or so primitive a device as that of Professor Petrie. From Herodotus' description one infers that the actual building of the pyramid itself, such as we see it now, did not offer any very extraordinary features ; it was the application of the casing alone that was a novelty and required machinery. Diodorus says in so many words that the pyramid was built by inclined planes, and that must have been the easiest way of doing it. It is somewhat startling, perhaps,

FIG. X.   POLYSPASTON OF THE TIME OF VITRUVIUS.

to contemplate the great pyramid from the Mena house which lies to the north of it, and think what an inclined plane, reaching to even half the height, must have been ; but if one can imagine one's self at the point of view of an Oriental despot the case would be different. Of the 3,000 Hindu temples in the district of Tanjore in Southern India, the most important is the huge edifice dating from the fourteenth century, A.D., in the city of Tanjore itself. The central tower of this great temple is 208 feet high and 96 feet square at the base. The huge circular dome at the top is a granite monolith, and from personal observation I should say that it weighs more than the largest stone in the pyramid of Cheops. According to Mr. W. S. Caine, a most interesting and reliable writer on Indian travel, "a local tradition says that an inclined plane of five miles in length was built, up which this enormous stone was rolled to the top of the tower, by forced labour." Five miles would have been an unnecessary length ; but the tradition is only five hundred years old, and that is the main point, for it comes well within the period of application of all the mechanical powers in India ; whatever might have been their early Indian history they were all brought to the banks of the Indus by Alexander, B.C. 326.

A heap or pile is the simplest of all architec-

E

tural objects and is the instinctive form of monument for mankind to erect in all ages. The savage builds his cairn of stones, a Tamerlane his heap of skulls, an Alyattus his tumulus larger than the tomb of Cheops: but it is in the solid square stone pyramid that the mechanic arts may first be said to come into play. It is a shape which lends itself to the use of the simplest mechanical appliances and, unlimited human labour being given, the appliances of the present time would be of small advantage to the architect. Supposing that to-day one had to reconstruct the pyramid of Cheops, the road and ferry from the quarry being in working order, and the floor plan having been laid out at one thousand feet from the edge of the plateau. Obviously the first lot of stones would be hauled directly to the pyramid site and, after being dressed, arranged in place by gangs of men with hand-spikes. So far as we now know, the only thing that would have to be looked out for on this ground floor would be a hole about four feet square at about one hundred and forty-two feet from the northern edge, where a passage commenced, extending to the blind pit about one hundred feet below the floor. The second course of stones would now be taken in hand, and the following question arises: Would one locate lifting machines or men with blocks and spars round this vast platform of thirteen and a half acres, and lift the next lot of stones bodily to the top of the first course and then move them to their proper positions ? or would it not be easier to extend the inclined plane from the edge of the plateau to the top of the first course, a height of about five feet, and haul the stones directly to their proper places ? There can be but one answer to the question put in this form, and that would be in favour of the inclined plane, and the process can be continued tier upon tier until the space on top of the truncated pyramid becomes so contracted that the large bodies of men hauling the stones cannot be handled there. There is no limit to the length of the inclined plane in order to maintain a hauling angle for the men, and the plane would be used as long as any of the stones were too heavy to be lifted bodily by any rapid working machine known at the time. The method of lifting on wooden blocks by means of levers would not have been practical because the equilibrium of heavy weights thus handled rapidly becomes unstable and dangerous, and at the edges of the pyramid many of the men with the levers would be in the same situation as Archimedes who could not lift the world because he had no place for a fulcrum to his lever. The polyspaston method would not have been used because, as shown by Queen Hatasoo's boat, the ancient Egyptians probably had no idea beyond the single pulley, and the number of men required for it could be worked to much better advantage on an inclined plane.   The fact that each pyramid had its own inclined causeway from the Nile valley to the plateau is strong presumptive evidence that it was intended to prolong that incline to the pyramid itself, because otherwise it would have been simpler to have used the Cheops incline always and to have dragged the stones for the second and third pyramid round the corner of the first pyramid and across the plateau to their ultimate destination.   The inclined plane between the edge of the plateau and the pyramid site was probably built of Nile mud bricks, either sun-dried or fire-baked, and such chippings as came from dressing the stones on each pyramid floor as the terraces rose one upon another.   The height to which this inclined plane rose, or the length of it, can never be known except approximately. When it reached the same angle as the Herodotus plane so as to be a simple prolongation, it then reached the pyramid at the height of about forty feet from the base, and the large stones just above the mouth of the pyramid entrance are near this point.   Whatever its length, its height must have been at least two hundred feet for the heaviest stones are found there in the roof of the king's chamber. An inclined plane from the edge of the plateau to this point would have an angle of one to seven, and to drag a sixty ton stone up this angle would require even more than the nine hundred men that I have calculated for a grade of one to ten. That calculation was, however, a liberal one, and a few more men would suffice. In regard to this point a communication of Colonel Wilks, R.A., published in 1821, in the " Transactions of the Royal Society of Edinburgh" on the methods of the natives for raising the immense stones found in the walls of Indian temples is very interesting. " These stones are moved end foremost up an inclined plane of solid earth, of as small an angle with the horizon as circumstances admit, to the spot which they are to occupy in the wall. Long bamboo poles lashed to the stone at right angles with its length, and at such distances as merely to admit the efforts of rows of labourers between, constitute the chief means of propelling it, by main force, up the inclined plane, and its ascent is facilitated by means of rollers of small diameter, successively introduced under the stone, and prevented from sinking into the earth by rows of planks placed on each side of the stone parallel to the line of ascent. When it has ascended the desired height it is twisted horizontally round by similar means into its destined position." Whether the civilization, religion and arts of the Indians were Egyptian in origin, as is claimed by some authors and as is shown for example in bull worship, it is certain that in their simple methods of accomplishing heavy tasks they are astonishingly similar, and this method of moving large blocks is an instance. If we apply this method to the sixty ton stone before described, it would give a practical additional force of about 256 men arranged on sixteen spars lashed across it 18 inches apart, 128 men on each side. This would bring up the total number to 1,156 which would be ample. The area of the pyramid platform at this point is only one-third of what it is at the base, but it is still nearly 450 feet square, over four and a half acres, an ample space for working bodies of men. Another method suggests itself at this point as a means of overcoming a steep incline. It is the method of Paeonius the architect of the temple of Diana at Ephesus in the fifth century B.C. Wishing, according to Vitruvius, to transport a block measuring 12 × 8 × 6 feet, and weighing over forty tons, from the quarry to the temple, a distance of nearly two miles, he inclosed it in wood to form a cylinder and rolled it by means of a rope. Fig. xi., drawn from the description, will give an idea. Paeonius only wanted this block for the base of the statue of Apollo, but he here seems to have been the inventor of the " parbuckle," the simplest method of sailors for getting spars on board when there are no masts in the ship to which tackles can be hooked. The ends of two

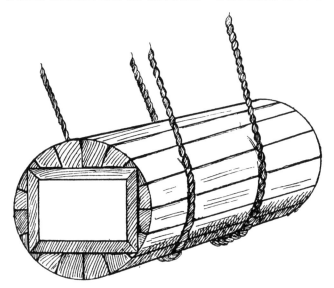

FIG. XI. PAEONIUS PARBUCKLE.

ropes being made fast on top of the pyramid platform, the other ends carried down the incline and brought back again and the cylindrically wood-padded stone placed in the loop or bight, the stone could be rolled up with less than half the force required to drag it on a sled; unfortunately for this theory, however, the Egyptians apparently did not understand the value of a pulley attached to the object to be moved, as was shown in discussing Queen Hatasoo's boat. This being the case they would not have understood the advantage of the parbuckle, and they would have been more likely to have lengthened out the inclined plane so as to make simple dragging less difficult.

Beside the inclined plane and handspike, the pyramid builders probably had some other mechanical appliances for lifting the casing stones and putting them in place. Herodotus distinctly says they had, but unfortunately his description, "a machine made of short pieces of wood," is utterly unintelligible because it lacks the essential element of a machine, *i.e.*, the source of power. There must be a lever or a spring or a screw or some other motive force before an assemblage of pieces of wood becomes a machine. In his description something very essential has been left out either by himself or his translators, and he appears himself to be in some doubt about the apparatus, for he says that it was described to him in two ways. It is not surprising if the accounts of the priests were somewhat vague, considering that the legend was 3,300 years old when Herodotus heard it, and possibly had no more foundation in fact than the goat story about the Chinese wall. A finished

casing stone, fig. xii., weighing from fifteen tons
to one, would be an awkward object to handle at
best, and it may have been necessary to clamp
it into some kind of a wooden cradle for the

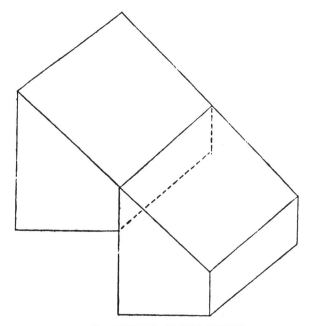

FIG. XII. FINISHED CASING STONES.

lifting machine to get hold of it, or it might have
been necessary to have had a succession of
cradles on each step of the pyramid in which to
land it in order that the next lifting machine
could take hold and a final landing cradle in

which it could be slid sidewise on the step of
the pyramid with its end exposed to make joint
with its predecessor. A pair of cranes with a
swinging arm or jib, capable of a short vertical
motion, mounted on each step, would be a
satisfactory means of lifting the casing blocks
and swinging them into place, or, indeed, to use
anywhere about the pyramid, but history fails
us when we seek authority on the subject so far
back as this, though, as before mentioned, Colonel
Vyse says he found holes for machinery of some
sort.   Thucydides, B.C. 470, mentions a swinging
lever, and Livy, B.C. 59, says that cranes were
invented in the time of Servius Tullius, the sixth
king of Rome, B.C. 560.   They form a variety
of the Charchefium described by Vitruvius as
used by the Greeks and Romans, and the idea
of such a machine for assisting in building the
pyramid is very natural on account of its simplicity.   In a curious book called "The Origin of
the Laws, Arts and Sciences and their Progress
among the Ancient Peoples from the Deluge to
the Death of Jacob;" by Antoine Goguet, published in Paris in 1758, the author suggests this
idea for the building of the entire pyramid, and
gives a large woodcut to illustrate his ideas.
His machine consists of a simple frame upon
the top of which is a beam pivoting on its
centre : one end of the beam is attached to a

stone and a number of men pull down on a rope
attached to the other. Goguet had evidently
never been in Egypt and had no idea of the
size of the stones to be lifted, and he makes no
mention in his book of where the idea came
from : but the principle is correct. According
to Murray's handbook of Syria, there was lately
found at Selkhat in the Hauran, the remains of
such a machine. "A tripod with wooden legs
60 feet high, on top was a lever of the first
order, of wood bolted and strapped with iron,
each arm 80 feet long and the lever capable of
horizontal movement, at one end were a series
of large claws for seizing the stones, at the
other a basket in which small stones could be
put to counterbalance." Diligent inquiry of the
Druses and Turks of Selkhat on the part of
later travellers has failed to produce any con-
firmation of the story ; but this does not render
it any the less probable, as from personal experience I am aware that, in remote regions, the
natives seldom know anything about the relics
of an older civilization. The machine was,
however, most probably a war machine for lifting a body of men across a ditch or to the top
of a wall, for Selkhat was a Roman castle surrounded by a moat, and located on the site of a
still older one. The construction of the machine
was not strong enough to have admitted of lift-

ing heavy stones owing to the beam resting on
top of the tripod.

In my opinion the humble shadoof, fig. ii.,
affords exactly the kind of machine used by the

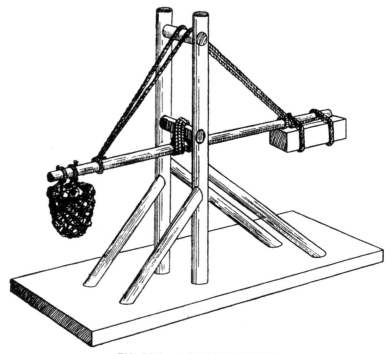

FIG. XIII.   A SHADOOF CRANE.

Egyptians.   Replace the pole and bucket at one
end of the beam by a rope-sling for a stone ;
replace the ball of mud at the other end by a
rope-basket or net into which small stones can

be thrown, and we have a machine whose every feature and principle we know them to have been acquainted with, and which they could make as strong as wood and rope, without iron, would allow, fig. xiii.   Some writers on Egypt refer to the crude forms of rope which the early Egyptians must have had, but this is a mistake.   Even the South Sea Islanders make good rope, and it may also be said that rope making marks the first stage of civilization where man improved upon the thong, cut from the raw hide or sinew of an animal.   In the Babylonian expedition of the University of Pennsylvania in 1892 there was found under the temple of Bel, the ruins of a drain with a key-stone arch, and in it a vase of terra cotta with a rope pattern on the exterior. The vase Dr. Hilprecht places at 5000 B.C., and also the arch and the weight of authority nowadays supposes the Egyptians to have come from that part of the world.   The pictured boats in the tomb of Ti, V. Dyn., and especially those of Queen Hatasoo, figs. iv. and v., show an immense amount of knowledge of rope making and rope using.   Several ancient specimens of rope made from the fibre of the date palm have been found in Egypt; but it is not surprising that more have not been discovered, for "dry rot," that peculiar enemy of ropes made of vegetable fibre, must have been very prevalent in that country. Undoubtedly they must have had still stronger ropes of raw hide and human hair, which were much in use by all ancient nations, women's hair being particularly in request for the twisted ropes of catapults, on account of its fineness and strength. Even to-day one can see in the new Hongwonje temple of Kioto, Japan, great coils of rope whose fibre has been contributed voluntarily by pious women throughout the Empire. The ancient Egyptians had also the knowledge of the use of many rope supports for a weak spar, as is shown by the multitude of lifts on the slender lower yard of Queen Hatasoo's boat. This kind of support would be necessary in the case of the shadoof lifting machine to enable it to lift a weight of five or six tons, and it could never have been able to do much more than that, for wood and rope have their limits, and this simple form of lever is a very poor one mechanically, the strain on it being double the weight to be lifted. The fore and main yards of an old fashioned frigate could lift from ten to twelve tons when working together, and it is not probable that the ancient Egyptians could have done better. Iron and steel cranes or derricks are absolutely necessary to lift and swing such great stones as are to be found in the pyramid, and the ancient Egyptians had no iron for structural purposes, for Professor

Petrie states that iron was very little used before B.C. 800, and none has ever been found except in the shape of tools, clamps and other small objects. Such cranes being wanting, the necessity is apparent of an inclined plane at least as high as the point where the roofing stones are found over the king's chamber. That such a machine as I have imagined would have been of great convenience anywhere about the pyramid platform, as it rose on each successive stage, is evident, especially at the edges where men could only work with hand-spikes on one side of a stone. Indeed, but for Herodotus' statement that the casing was put on from the top downward, one can hardly see why it was not done the other way, and the whole pyramid, casing and all, finished at each stage, excepting in the part next the inclined plane, which part would of course be finished as the inclined plane was taken down. It would be interesting to take off a casing stone from one of the other pyramids to see if one could discover how the lifting machine took hold of it. Possibly nothing would be found, for the Egyptians, Greeks and Romans usually left projections for this purpose, which were afterwards cut off when the stone was in place, though the operation would have been very awkward with a casing stone. Other methods were also sometimes adopted. In the sandstone quarries of Silsilis,

500 miles above Cairo, there was found a sculpture representing some tools employed by the quarrymen; two of these are apparently wedges, but the other is a metal eye-bolt let into a hole in a stone and secured there temporarily by a removable wedge. This method is described also by Vitruvius, and there is an American invention called a Lewis bolt, for use in ships' decks, which is the same thing. In the Greek temples at Girgenti in Sicily, fifth century B.C., built of a soft stone, grooves are cut in the shape of a horse-shoe in each stone at the joining surface of the ends. Each stone could thus be swung to exactly the place it was to occupy, and the rope strap passing round the horse-shoe withdrawn. These temples are on the top of steep hills, and no inclined planes were reasonably possible.

If we admit that the pyramid builders could have had such machines as I have described, it then becomes possible to consider their use in the building of the whole pyramid above the 200 foot stage. When this point has been reached, about 5,400,000 tons will have been placed, and there remains only about 1,340,000 tons or one-fifth of the whole pyramid to complete it. To carry an inclined plane to the top of the pyramid at a grade of one in ten, it would be necessary to commence it 6,000 feet away in the Nile valley at a point (9) over 1,600 feet before the commencement of the Herodotus incline, fig. ix.

In addition to the Herodotus incline I have considered also as necessary the plane reaching from the edge of the plateau to the 200 foot level. In order to carry these two planes up to the plane reaching to the top of the pyramid, 75,000,000 cubic feet of Nile bricks would be necessary, or four times the number of cubic feet of stone still required to finish the pyramid. Of course this rise in the plane would take place gradually, but there would always be four times as much work to do on the inclined plane as on the pyramid. The labour consideration would not enter the problem, since there was so much of it ; but the time element involved in finishing the pyramid would always have been of importance, for it is not likely that Cheops could have had much confidence in the zeal of Cephren, his successor, to finish his pyramid when Cephren had his own to think about. Under these circumstances it is reasonable to suppose that when the stones grew light enough for the machines to compete with the inclined plane, the latter was stopped. In connection with these shadoof cranes there might have been capstans or windlasses, provided Viollet le Duc is right in dating saqquiehs from the earliest dynasties, but they do not appear to have been essential.   There is still, however, one point that I have not been able to clear up, and that is, how the pyramid builders were able to move the very heavy blocks of granite in the confined spaces that are sometimes found, particularly according to Professor Petrie, in the second and third pyramids, for it seems quite impossible that everything could have been built in place as each course of the pyramid was completed.   The movement required may have been only a few inches; but there is no space for any motive power except a hydraulic or screw jack.   It has been urged by many writers that the ancient Egyptians must have possessed inventions of which we have no knowledge; but in all other parts of the world the human mind has developed in but one way in regard to the mechanical sciences, and there is no reason to suppose that the Egyptian mind developed in any other way.   It is more probable that they possessed many inventions which we have since re-discovered, the intervening connecting thread of information having been lost.   Necessity has been the mother of invention with us, and it must have been the same with them.   The screw jack or press affords an excellent example of this matter of re-invention.   As before stated, the dark age of Europe, from the fifth to the ninth centuries, A.D., lost to us nearly everything that was useful in the mechanic arts, and when more peaceful times enabled the peasants of France and Germany to cultivate the vine, they were for ages without the means of pressing the grapes except by treading. First came the clumsy lever wine press, and this was succeeded by the screw wine press in the south of France about 1685. But when the stored literature of the convents came to be re-discovered we find Vitruvius, who knew all about the screw press, and when we discover the Greek authors we find that Archimedes was the inventor, and he was educated in Egypt. Pascal also invented the hydraulic press in 1650, but when we get back to the Greeks we find that its invention lies between Archimedes, Hero, and Ctesibus, who were graduates from the same school. How any mechanical information possessed by the ancient Egyptians could have been lost to the Greeks is beyond comprehension, because not only has history shown that the knowledge of the mechanic arts degenerates slower than any other knowledge possessed by a declining nation : but there are examples in Egypt where exactly the same things were done from the earliest dynasties down to the latest without any break in the continuity. For instance, Apis or bull worship is traced back to Ka-Kau the II King of the II Dyn., B.C. 4100,

and was continued to 50 B.C. I have been
unable to find any record of their precise
method of burial before B.C. 1600; but at this
time the huge stone sarcophagus was lowered
into a deep pit sunk in the solid rock, which
method was continued down to B.C. 1100, when
a system of tunnelling was introduced, which
method continued down to the time of the later
Ptolemies, B.C. 50. A visit to this Apis
mausoleum in the Saqqarah desert is very
interesting from a mechanical point of view.
As shown in fig. xiv, the vaults lie on both
sides of the tunnel, but never opposite; the
average size of a sarcophagus is 13 feet long,
11 high, and 7½ wide, and the weight 65 tons;
the floor of the vault is three or four feet below
that of the tunnel, and the width and length of
the vault are only about two or three feet greater
than the sarcophagus itself.   In the tunnel lies
a sarcophagus nearly blocking it up; it was left
there by one of the viceroys [who had taken it
from its vault] on account of the mechanical
difficulty of removing it to the museum at Cairo.
Except in the tunnel there is absolutely no room
to work a gang of men or to use either lever,
wheel and axle, pulley, inclined plane or wedge,
nothing in fact but the screw or hydraulic jack.
There is not a hole or a projection either on
the sides, roof or floor of the tunnel, vault or

sarcophagus. The entire mechanical surround-
ings call for the jack and nothing else, and the
very fact that the vaults do not come opposite
each other is almost positive proof that a jack
was used, because a solid wall was necessary to
push against. The point to which I wish to
draw particular attention in this matter is that
the same kind of work had been going on here
for 800 years before Archimedes was in Egypt,
and was continued for 200 years after he left

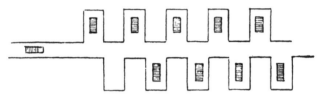

FIG. XIV. PLAN OF APIS MAUSOLEUM, SAQQARAH.

the country, the locality was less than 150 miles
from his university, and the two places are connected by water.

The mechanical problems in connection with
the construction of the pyramid of Cheops are
interesting, but the executive ability shown by
its constructor is more to be admired than the
mechanical problems which that ability was
able to overcome. Professor Rawlinson thinks
that Cheops must have been divinely inspired
simply to conceive of so wonderful a creation,
so absolutely perfect in all its parts; but the

man who was able to carry out the conception is deserving of more credit than he, for few men could have had a more difficult task since the world was created. To plan the great work, to lay it out, to provide for all possible emergencies and accidents, to see that the men were all continuously and profitably employed, that the means of transportation was ample and always in order, that the commissariat did not fail, that the water supply was ample and conveniently disposed, that the sick reliefs were on hand, that the master workmen were not discontented, the journeymen not idle, and the apprentices well disciplined; combine all these and many other sources of care and irritation with the inconveniences and interruptions of a cumbersome religion, whose ceremonies must have continually interfered with the prosecution of a religious work such as this was, and we have a sum total which would tax the ablest organizer that has ever lived.

CHAPTER IV.

THE exact method by which the ancient Egyptians were able to quarry any kind of stone from the softest to the hardest is unknown, because both Greeks and Romans have continued work in the same localities, and it is impossible to distinguish the traces from each other. Although De Roziere, Belzoni, Kircher, and others have imagined the ancients to have had powerful and unknown machinery for chiseling and breaking away huge blocks from a quarry face, there is no proof of it, and the principal methods followed were probably the simple ones pursued in India in our own time, which are ample for all the conditions involved. These are of two kinds, one depending upon fire the other upon percussion, and at Assouan and Shellal are evidences of each. The first is described by Sir J. F. Herschell as follows: "The workman marks on the stone a line in the direction of the intended separation, along which a groove is cut with a chisel, about a couple of inches in depth. Above this groove a narrow line of fire is then kindled and maintained till the rock below is thoroughly heated, immediately on which a line of men and women, each provided with a pot full of cold water, suddenly sweep off the ashes and pour the water into the heated groove, when the rock at once splits with a clear fracture." The second method is thus given by Col. Wilks: " The workman looks for a plain naked surface of sufficient extent, and a stratum of the proper thickness sufficiently near to the edge of the rock to facilitate the separation, or made so by previous trimming. The spot being determined, a line is marked along the direction of the intended separation, and a groove, about two inches wide and deep, is cut with chisels; or if the substratum be thin, holes of the same dimensions, at one and one half feet or two feet distant, are cut along the line. In either case all being now ready, a workman with a small chisel is placed at each hole or interval, and with small iron mallets the line of men keep beating on the chisels, but not with violence, from left to right or from right to left; this operation, as they say, is sometimes continued for two or three days before the separation is effected." There is also to be seen at Assouan evidences of the possibilities of another method which was suggested by Wilkinson, and seems to be universally accepted as the most plausible. This consists of the long groove described by Herschel and Wilks as being used in India; but it has, at intervals in it, chisel holes; these holes are thought by Wilkinson, De Morgan, and others to have been intended for dry wooden wedges which, after being driven into the holes, were swelled by water poured into the groove, the rock being split by the expansion of the wedges. I have examined many of these grooves, and the holes appear to be so shallow and tapering, that a wooden wedge would back out as soon as it commenced to swell. Many of the grooves also are on an inclined surface, where water could not be kept in them even by damming. From a somewhat intimate acquaintance with Asiatics and the minute character of the precautions to be taken to ensure that no mistakes are made by these human machines, I am inclined to the opinion that Colonel Wilks' method was the one employed, and that the holes were placed in the groove in order that each one in the row of workmen might know exactly where to place his chisel when the stone was to be split.

As to the tools used by the ancient Egyptians, they were of flint, bronze, and iron, and all three have continued in use down to the present. One explorer, even during the nineteenth century, having found an old man in his party of

native followers who shaved his head in a most
unsatisfactory fashion with a flint razor, while
his up-to-date grandsons used Sheffield steel.
Very few iron tools have been found, probably
because of its rapid oxidation, as the soil of
Egypt is specially nitrous. A small piece of
plate iron, now in the British Museum, was
found in one of the air passages of the great
pyramid by Colonel Vyse, and also some iron
clamps which secured one of the stones in
position where two passages join, and a few
iron tools are to be found in the large museums
of Europe.   Herodotus says also that the pyramid workmen had iron tools, or rather he mentions iron tools, among other items, in speculat-
ing on the cost of the pyramid.   Apparently the
ancients had either steel tools or some method
of tempering bronze unknown to us, because of
the marvellous precision and finish with which
hieroglyphics and other ornaments are cut upon
the hardest monuments.   M. Le Bas, who was
detained some time at Luxor while waiting the
rising of the Nile before floating down the Paris
obelisk, made some careful experiments, which
are worth noting.   He says that Egyptian
granite can be cut easily enough with modern
chisels, making light blows, and the chisel lasts
half a day ; time alone is required : quick cutting blunts the chisel immediately.   The hiero-

glyphics, he says, are simply picked out with a pointed tool, and under the microscope the curved surfaces present a continuation of small circumferences, of which the asperities have been rubbed down in polishing the granite. This is extremely interesting in connection with the following extract from a communication of Dr. Kennedy to the "Edinburgh Philosophical Journal," in 1821, on the subject of working and polishing granite in India: "I shall subjoin some notices of the manner in which I have seen the hardest granite cut by Hindoo workmen. The only tools which they employ are a small steel chisel and an iron mallet . . . the chisel tapers to a round point like that of a drawing pencil, and this, I believe, is the only shape ever given to the points of their chisels." The mallet, he says, only weighs a few pounds, and the striking face has a hollow in it which is lined with lead. "With these simple tools even the gigantic granite fortress of Dowlatabad and the wonderful caverns at Ellora were carried out." The Egyptians, however, were not confined to this one shaped chisel. Wilkinson found a bronze one among limestone chippings in a tomb at Thebes which had an edge $\frac{7}{8}$ of an inch wide. The head was turned over from long use, but the edge was perfectly sharp; yet he adds: "the point is now easily turned by striking it against the very stone it was made to cut." Probably time alone had drawn its temper. Professor Petrie is of opinion that bronze tools with diamond teeth were used by the pyramid builders both in the form of saws and hollow drills, and he makes an able argument in favour of this view. Whatever the nature of the tools, they certainly bored holes in the hardest stone with some kind of a hollow drill, and afterwards broke off the core. An example of this can be seen at Karnak, near the lotus columns of Thothmes III., B.C. 1503, before the sanctuary, and another example is at the Lion's gate in the old citadel of Mycenæ in Greece, B.C. 1100. This one is remarkable in another respect. There are two holes drilled overhead in a corner of the door lintels, where there is no room to have made the revolution of an ordinary drill brace, and some kind of a ratchet must have been used.

Apparently all statues, obelisks, sarcophagi, etc., were finished at the quarry before transportation, except, perhaps, the polishing and cutting of hieroglyphics. With the clumsy methods of transportation in vogue, any excess of weight must have been an important matter, but the primary reason was most likely because the weather was always pleasant and the work could as well be done in the open air at the

quarry as anywhere else, and if flaws were discovered the piece could be rejected then and
there.   The unfinished statue of Amen-hetep
III. at Shellal is probably an example, and the
unfinished obelisk at Assouan (fig. xv.), undoubtedly is; the flaw can be seen, though it is
not visible in the illustration.   The marks there
shown are grooves made at some later date with
the intention of cutting it up.   This obelisk is
95 feet long and 11 feet 1½ inches square at the
base, and would form one of the most interesting
sights in Egypt if it were kept properly cleared
of sand by the authorities.   A stone of this size
that has lain in a quarry for 3,000 years and
which looks as if the workmen had only left for
the day and would be back again to-morrow,
should be something quite impressive.   As it
is, however, it is very disappointing.   Whatever
methods the Egyptians may have adopted for
extracting ordinary blocks it is evident that in
this particular case they could have made use of
neither of the Indian methods that I have described, because the stone has been laboriously
cut free on three sides and remains attached
only by its under side to the bed rock.   Regarding the final detachment, Wilkinson thinks that
spaces were cut underneath which were filled
with wood and the remaining rock supports cut
away, leaving the obelisk resting on the wood.

Probably the sled on which it was to be transported was built under it at this time. We
know from the sculpture at Deir-el-Bahri of the
transport of an obelisk on a boat (fig. xvii.), that
it rested on a sled, and this would have been
the most favourable time for putting the obelisk
upon it. It is seldom that one sees a more
striking evidence of what can be accomplished
by patient, unremitting toil than is afforded by
this obelisk ; but many writers are disposed to
think that it is in itself a larger object than
would be undertaken nowadays even with the
aid of modern explosives; but this is far from
being the case. Only last year, according to
the U.S. " Industrial Journal," a block of
granite was blown without fracture from the
quarry of Redstone, N. H., which was 145 feet
long, 35 feet wide, and 28 feet deep, a mass
more than twelve times as large as this Assouan
obelisk. Though the ancients were faultlessly
accurate in fitting granite blocks together, for
some unknown reason they were not always so
particular in cutting the sides of their obelisks.
It has been found that the two obelisks of
Luxor, which were more accurately measured
than any others, are crooked—the one in Paris
being a little more so than the remaining one.
Two of the sides of both obelisks are flat, but
the other two swell out over an inch and a

FIG. XV. UNFINISHED OBELISK AT ASSOUAN.

quarter : both as they originally stood at Luxor had the swelled sides in a N.W. and S.E. direction, and the centre of each obelisk was curved half an inch in a N.W. direction. Possibly this warping might happen to any stone taken fresh from the quarry and placed on end in the broiling sun of Egypt. The Paris obelisk was a little smaller than the other, and was placed half a diameter in advance, so that to a person approaching by the sphinx avenue leading to the temple they would look exactly the same. That the Paris obelisk was ever taken away is much to be regretted, for Luxor is the only temple in Egypt in which temple, pylon, statues, and obelisks still occupied their original positions.

In the matter of polishing granite the ancient Egyptians were unexcelled. Le Bas says that he found from experiment that sandstone, pumice stone, and time are all the elements required, and Dr. Kennedy describes a method practised in India which also seems reasonable. The stone having been brought to a surface by the chisel, is then water-dressed in the manner usual to masons. " It now only remains to apply the black shining polish, which is done as follows : A block of granite of considerable size is rudely fashioned into the shape of the end of a large pestle. The lower face of this is hollowed out into a cavity, and this is filled with a mass composed of powered corundum stone, mixed with melted beeswax.   This block is moved by means of two sticks or pieces of bamboo, placed one on each side of the neck, and bound together by cords, twisted and tightened by sticks.   The weight of the whole is as much as two workmen can easily manage.   They seat themselves upon or close to the stone they are to polish and, by moving the block backwards and forwards between them, the polish is given by the friction of the mass of wax and corundum. . . . It would appear that the polish thus given to granite may be said to be as imperishable as the material itself to which it is applied. . . . In the end of the year 1794 I had an opportunity of visiting the ancient city of Warankul and of seeing a granite gateway, standing within the bounds of the palace, the fine black polish of which appeared to have lost nothing of its original lustre. . . . The gateway in question could scarcely have been less than 500 years old, and might probably have been considerably older."

CHAPTER V.

BOTH naval constructor Le Bas, who transported and erected the Paris obelisk in 1832, and Lieut.-Comdr. Gorringe, who transported and erected the New York obelisk in 1880, have written most interesting accounts of their own operations, and have made exhaustive historical research as to what had previously been done; both agreed that the ancient Egyptians must have had mechanical appliances equal in efficiency to any that we now possess; but both failed to find any proof of their opinion except in the extreme difficulty of the work itself. Since their day nothing further has been brought to light which bears upon the subject, except the discovery by M. Naville at Deir el Bahri, of the sculpture of the transport of two obelisks on a boat (fig. xvii.). Since the cuts were made for the Archæological Report of the Egypt Exploration Fund, from which these figures are taken, more remnants of the sculpture have been discovered, and among others, most fortunately, is one from the middle of the boat, and it shows

G

the two obelisks stowed base to base lengthwise
of the boat, instead of alongside each other as
shown in fig. xviii.   By this sculpture the following points have been cleared up.   First:
extremely heavy weights were transported by
water, though Wilkinson and some other writers
believe that they were always transported by
land.   Second : a regularly-built barge or lighter
was used, which must have been at least 12
feet high out of water and 250 feet long, with
pointed ends, and not a low pontoon raft.
Third : the Egyptians must have discovered
by former experience that if they stowed the
obelisks end to end, the vessel could be nar-
rower, and would thus be more manageable in
a current than if the obelisks were carried
parallel to each other as shown, which neces-
sitates more beam.   That the wider boat had
already been tried is to be inferred from a text
given by M. Naville, showing that in the reign
of Thothmes I., the father of Hatasoo, one Anna
had brought down two obelisks on a boat 200
feet long and 69 feet wide.   The width of this
boat is one-third the length, and as the remaining obelisk of Thothmes I. at Karnak is 93
feet high, a length of 200 feet would not be
sufficient for two such, end to end, and allow a
margin for the taper and rise of the bow and
stern.   Fourth : they knew that a vessel so con-

structed would " hog " or droop at the ends, as
the centre only would be waterborne, and they
invented the rainbow truss, which we thought a
brilliant American idea, when the shallow water
of the Mississippi necessitated a similar invention for large steamers, and it was called a " hog
frame." This rope truss can be seen to better
advantage in fig. v. All of Queen Hatasoo's Punt
boats were supplied with it. There it is nearly
as large as a man's waist, and so much larger
than was used on board modern ships before
the days of wire rope and chain, that there are
no tables for calculating its strength. Approximately, on the basis of Manilla hemp, it would
stand the strain of over 300 tons. It will be
noted in fig. xvii., that there is a small picture
of an obelisk on a boat, marked O, just above
the large obelisk; this is the determinative
sign attached to the hieroglyphic name of the
boat, and apparently is symbolical merely, as it
simply represents half the boat, with a stern
and rudder attached to it, and cuts the rainbow
truss in the middle. Curiously enough, however, it shows exactly how the lashings were
passed under the obelisk and over the truss, the
weight of the obelisks thus pulling the middle
of the truss down and lifting the bow and stern.
In 1834 there were found at the Piræus some
marble tablets, being what we would call to-day

the "book of allowances" of the ancient Athenian fleet; among other articles are mentioned a "hypozomata," which formed a part of the gear of every ship, and was stored on shore when she was laid up in the dockyard. It was a rope which went from end to end of the ship, but neither Professor Bökh, the translator of the Attic tables, nor Graser, Schaeffer, Jal, Le Roy, Bloomfield or any other modern writer has been able to give a clear idea of its use, though Isadore, a Spanish writer of the seventeenth century, says that there was in ancient ships a rope going from end to end, and called a "tormentum," because it was twisted. Every one seemed to think it was a rope like a fender, going round the gunwale just under the rail, and older writers, like Hesychius and Polybius, were no clearer, though Athenæus says there was a hypozomata on board the great ship of Ptolemy Philopeter, which was 483 feet long, and was built B.C. 300. Smith in his "Voyage and Shipwreck of St. Paul," 1848, for the first time advances the theory that because the ancient Greek ships were so long and had such heavy rostra and towers at each end, the hypozomata might have been a rope between the high stem and stern post, which was twisted in the same manner as the rope of a catapult. It has remained for the walls of Deir el Bahri to show that there was such a rope and how it was applied 1,300 years before the time of the most ancient Greek records.

Fifth : we discover that obelisks were entirely completed at the quarry, they were not sheathed in wood for protection, and no holes were made or excrescences left, as some have supposed, to assist in handling. It is noticeable that in Rome all the obelisks have holes in them, which were probably found necessary by the engineers to secure their tackles, etc. Sixth : it was strapped with rope, having eyes spliced in the ends next the pyramidon, showing that part of the pulling force was applied here. Seventh : the obelisk was dragged on a sled in the same simple manner as were the smallest objects, as shown in the tomb pictures. Eighth : the obelisks were put on board the vessel sidewise. It would have been impossible to do so lengthwise on account of the shape of the bow and stern, and the rope truss.

These two obelisks were, according to inscriptions still extant, quarried, transported from Assouan 135 miles to Karnak, and erected in the space of seven months, which all writers consider as something marvellous : but it must be remembered that a superintendent and a working force of men must have been continually employed at the Assouan quarry, not only because penal servitude in the quarries was the usual form of punishment for both political and civil offences, but because it must have been necessary to keep the quarry free from sand. This superintendent would have been constantly prospecting the site for obelisk blocks in order to find localities free from flaws, all ready to commence work upon, even if he did not keep ready cut obelisks in stock. Governments were not different in those days from what they are now, and when a government wants anything it wants it in a hurry, as every contractor and executive officer is aware. Besides, with such a climate as Egypt has, night work would have been as easy as day work, and the seven months would practically be fourteen.

One of these obelisks was 105 feet high, the other 98, and the weight of each about 374 tons. The former is still standing. Doubtless the whole story of the quarrying, land transport and erection was told in sculpture at Deir el Bahri; but it has nearly all disappeared.

The only illustration that has ever been found in Egypt descriptive of the transportation of a heavy object on land, is the celebrated " Colossus on a sledge," fig. xvi., which was found on the wall of a tomb at El Bersheh. For the purposes of my essay it is the most interesting discovery that has ever been made, because it shows

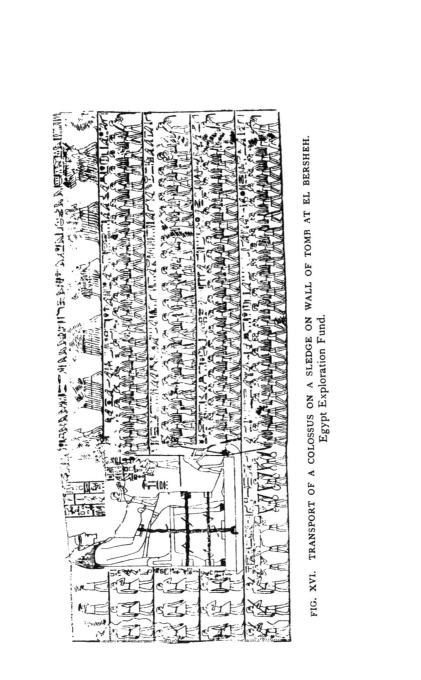

FIG. XVI. TRANSPORT OF A COLOSSUS ON A SLEDGE ON WALL OF TOMB AT EL BERSHEH.
Egypt Exploration Fund.

beyond a doubt that no labour saving machinery
whatever was employed in such cases, and we
can gather certain facts from the picture and
the hieroglyphic inscription, which enable us to
prove that the work was even more gigantic
than would appear at the first glance.   The text
of the inscription is said by all Egyptologists to
be extremely difficult to translate, but the main
facts, as translated by Chabas in 1873, so far as
they relate to my purposes, do not differ from
the later translations of Maspero, Erman,
Brugsch or Newberry.   The tomb belonged
to a gentleman named Kai, who lived in the
XII. Dynasty, B.C. 2466, and was of royal blood
on his mother's side ; he was also governor of
the town to which the Colossus was transported
from the quarry.   The work is described as a
tremendous undertaking, as indeed it must
have been, and all the inhabitants of the town
came out to meet it, while the women sang
songs in praise of the wonderful achievement.
" The old vied with the young, and each one
made the effort of a thousand." Chabas says
that the eighty-four men in seven groups in the
upper part of the picture, who look like soldiers,
consist of recruits to make the road, corporations
of sacred workmen, and stone cutters with their
masters ; while Mr. Newberry says, with regard
to the men dragging the statue, that the two

places of honour in the middle are reserved for the youths of the privileged military and sacerdotal class, while the two outer rows are occupied by the able bodied youths of the E. and W. side of the nome or district, and all in the four groups are represented by the inscription as giving their services joyfully in honour of their prince. Whatever they may be the three men with the rods look suspiciously like the cattle drivers in fig. viii. The inscription states that the statue is made of Alabaster or Arragonite, and is 13 cubits in height, or 22·4 feet, and it now becomes necessary to calculate the weight of this sitting figure with only this data, and the picture in profile as a base of operations. We proceed as follows. All illustrations of the Ancient Egyptians show them to have been rather a light built people with broad shoulders. It will be fair then to assume that they were on the average men of 5 feet 6 inches in height when standing, and consequently about 4 feet high when sitting, with shoulders 18 inches across. The weight would be about 145 lbs. The latest and probably the most exact copy of the Colossus picture is that of Mr. Newberry, whose plan and measurements were made by Mr. Fraser in 1892, published by the Egypt Exploration Fund (El Bersheh, part i., plate xv.), and in this copy the length of the foot of the Colossus is 1·5 inch, the same as the average height of the men on the drag ropes or 5·5 feet. If the figure were standing, it would be 30·8 feet high and 8·4 feet broad across the shoulders. Since similar solids are to each other in proportion to the cubes of their like dimensions, an Egyptian 30·8 feet high would weigh 11·4 tons. If this Egyptian were placed in water and his lungs filled with it as in drowning, he would just sink, showing that his weight is slightly heavier than an equal bulk of water, *i.e.*, his specific gravity is about 1010; but the specific gravity of alabaster is 2700, and therefore the weight of the figure in alabaster would be 31·8 tons. But beside the figure there is the chair upon which it is sitting, and the base upon which the chair is resting, and, as is customary with Egyptian sitting statues, both are solid. Using the height of a man as a standard of measure we find that the square part of the chair, if 10 feet wide, measures 906 cubic feet, and as alabaster weighs 168·6 lbs. per cubic foot, its weight is 68 tons. The back of the chair in similar cases to be seen in the museums is most frequently only a support for the back of the figure, and in this case would be about 5 feet wide and would weigh 7 tons. The base is more than 19 feet long and would weigh 26 tons. Adding these weights together, we have a total weight of 132 tons on the sledge.

If instead of calculating the weight of the figure separately from that of the chair and base, we measure the whole solid mass, using as before the height of a man as a standard, we will find its weight to be a little over 140 tons. As, however, we cannot by this method allow for the various cavities, since we only have the profile and an estimated width upon which to base our calculations, it is fair to assume that the weight of 132 tons is the most accurate. The total number of men required to drag this weight, as previously explained in the case of the pyramid stone, would be 1,980, instead of the 172 that are attached to the drag ropes. It is difficult to explain this anomaly, unless there is something in the text which has not yet been properly translated, for average human strength has not changed since the days of the ancient Egyptians. The "Scientific American," than whom there is no better authority, says : " The limit of a man's walking pull is about 40 lbs. The utmost that he can pull by moving forward at a pulling angle that will keep him from slip- ping may be one-half his weight, say 75 lbs " ; and since the Egyptians were not equal to Europeans or Americans in physique, I have in my calculations used even a less estimate. The

whole of these 172 men pulling with a force of
40 lbs. each could not have dragged a Colossus
of more than one-ninth the size of that shown
on the sledge, and if exerting their utmost force
of 75 lbs. each, which would merely enable them
to start and not keep going, they could only
have moved one of one-fifth the size.   Chabas
and other early writers speak of the twelve men
in rear of the statue as "supernumeraries ready
to render assistance"; but Mr. Newberry, the
latest investigator, says that the inscription
shows that one of the men in the rear was the
sculptor and another a high steward.   However
this may be, I am inclined to the opinion that
there was perhaps some reason for putting exactly twelve men in rear, from the fact that
twelve times the 172 men at the drag ropes is
2,064, which is only 84 more than my estimate,
and that the painter having occupied with 172
men all the space allowed him could only indicate the remainder.   It is possible, also, that
what Chabas and others have translated about
each one making the effort of a thousand may
bear upon this point.

On the knee of the Colossus a man is seen
giving the step by clapping his hands.   The
object of the man in front is given a variety of
interpretations ; one thinks he may be throwing
something ; another, from the inscription, that

he is fanning incense ; to me it appears that he
is repeating the clapping of the timekeeper on
the knee by beating together a pair of hand
drums, such as one can still see in Egypt.
Mere hand-clapping would never have carried
the sound to the necessary distance, and keeping step was absolutely essential.   The exact
object of the notched log of wood carried by
three men is not clear, but Professor Petrie has
given a reasonable explanation in supposing it
to be used wherever there was a hole in the
road by being placed in front of the runner with
the notched side down to prevent it from slipping ; there was probably another on the other
side of the statue.   It is strange that there is
no sign of rollers or planks or corduroy road
bed, for a weight of 132 tons concentrated on a
base only 19 x 10 feet must have been very
difficult to manage ; but wood was doubtless
more valuable than man power, and it may be
that with broad runners, well lubricated with
oil as is shown, and operating upon fine sand, a
reasonable traction was obtained.

   If this primitive method of transportation was
resorted to in the case of Queen Hatasoo's
obelisks, and there seems to be no reason to
doubt it, a force of 5,585 men would have been
required, harnessed in double rank to four drag
ropes, as in the case of the pyramid stone ; they

would cover a space of about 1,400 feet, about twice the length of the most modern ocean steamer, with 1,396 men on each rope. There is no doubt that this force could drag the stone when they were once drilled to pull together, and here we have an excellent reason why in all the pictures, we see only men and not animals employed for hauling valuable wrought stones. Men can be drilled to march in absolute cadence to a song or timekeeping instrument, even when hauling a weight and a " one, two, three, and a surge " will produce a momentary force represented by nearly the weight of the whole mass of men, or several times their ordinary pulling force. Vacancies in the ranks caused by sickness can also be filled without materially affecting the drill of the remainder, and cattle can never be so well organized.

The embarkation was probably effected as follows. A dry dock was dug out at a short distance from the river bank at Assouan, in a position at right angles across the road along which the obelisks were to be dragged from the quarry. In this dock the lighter was built, and was afterward floated so that its deck was the exact height of the roadway. The obelisks were then hauled from the quarry and turned half round just before reaching the lighter, and launching skids were led to the deck. In this position 40 drag ropes could be made fast to the obelisk and led over the ship's deck to the roadway beyond, where 140 men could be harnessed to each, and the obelisk dragged on board.   The dike separating the dock from the Nile was then entirely cut away, and the lighter floated into the river.   When the boat reached Thebes the operation was reversed.   Capstans and screw or hydraulic jacks would have been extremely useful in all these operations, particularly for placing the obelisks in the exact centre line of the lighter, but they were not absolutely necessary as long as there was room to work all the men on the drag ropes and for the use of handspikes of sufficient length.

The water transport of these obelisks is most interesting.   Fig. xvii. shows a portion of the remains of the sculpture, and figs. xviii. xix. xx. show M. Naville's ingenious interpretation of it. In the sculpture the boats are arranged in three columns of ten boats each; both the boats and the columns are echelonned as in fig. v. because of the contracted space on the wall which was allowed to the sculptor.   Each boat had 32 rowers, making 320 in each column, or 960 in all.   On each side of the lighter was a small dispatch boat and in rear were three sacred boats, for an obelisk was a religious monument, and a pan of frankincense is placed upon it.   The lighter was steered by four rudders and the two rear boats in each column had two rudders. The steering must have been very bad, and possibly if the whole of the stern of the obelisk lighter could be found it would be seen that there were drags out astern to assist in keeping her head straight. They would be very efficient under such circumstances, and Herodotus says that they were in common use on the Nile in his day, B.C. 450.

Where objects larger than obelisks were transported, the problem of employing mere man power becomes more formidable. If we take, for example, the gritstone colossi of Amenhotep III., about B.C. 1420, in the plain of Thebes, figs. xxi. xxii., we find that each weighs from 800 to 1,000 tons or more than both the obelisks of Queen Hatasoo. According to Rawlinson, a text that has been found gives the following from the lips of the sculptor himself: " I caused to be built eight ships whereupon the statues were carried up the river; they were emplaced in their sublime temple ; they will last as long as heaven. A joyful event was it when they were landed at Thebes and raised up in their places." These eight ships must have constituted the floats of one or two pontoon rafts, each float having a carrying capacity of 250 tons or a total of 2,000 tons. As the weight of an ordinary

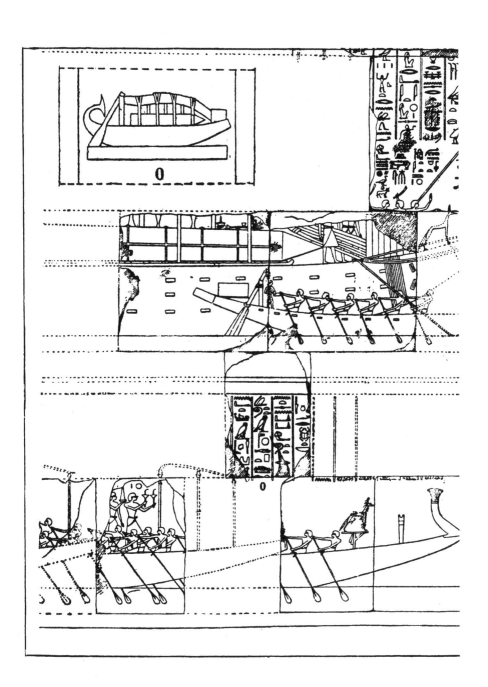

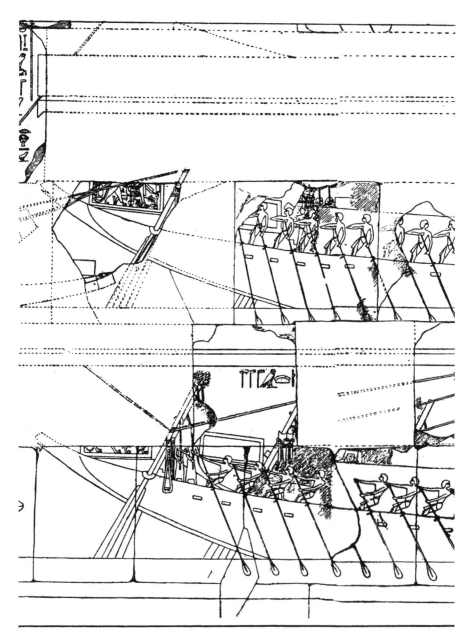

FIG. XVII. TRANSPORT OF OBELISKS. From a Bas-Relief of Deir el Bahri.

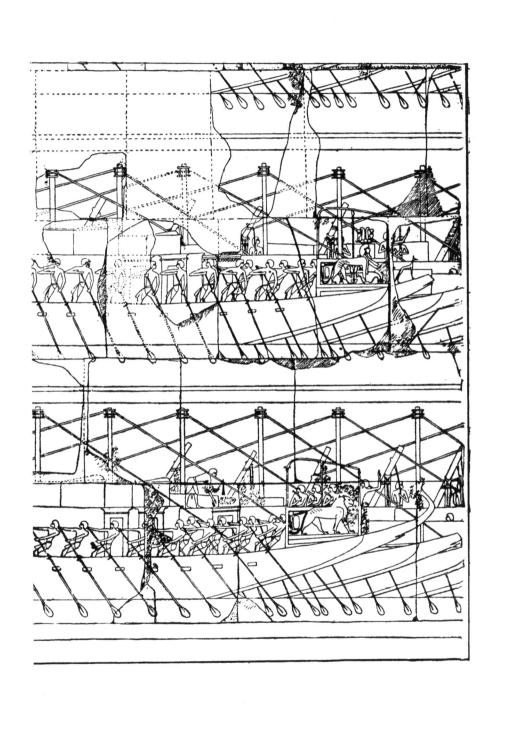

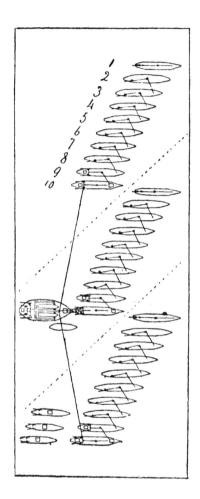

FIG. XVIII.
TRANSPORT OF AN OBELISK.
Egypt Exploration Fund.

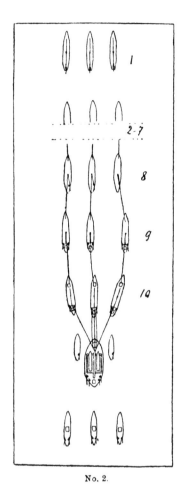

No. 2.

FIG. XIX.
TRANSPORT OF AN OBELISK
Egypt Exploration Fund.

FIG. XX.   TRANSPORT OF AN OBELISK.
Egypt Exploration Fund.

wooden ship is about 40 per cent. of its displacement, each would therefore be of about
420 tons, which would make a box lighter of
125 feet long, 40 feet wide and about 3 feet
draft. Four of these would measure 250 feet
long and 80 feet wide, and be suitable for one
colossus. Eight would measure 500 feet long
by 80 feet beam, and would carry both colossi
one behind the other. This may seem rather
long, but according to Diodorus, Rameses II.,
B.C. 1300, built a complete vessel, 283 cubits or
488 feet long, and, according to Wilkinson and
several other authors, Ptolemy Philopator,
B.C. 300, built one of the same length. In any
event it would have been almost as easy to tow
both pontoons as to tow one, and the two could
have been separated at awkward places in the
river. For the land transport of each of these
colossi about 15,000 men would have been
required; but there would be an advantage in
the disposition of the men over the case of the
obelisk in the fact that the base of the colossus
being so wide, 15 drag ropes could be attached
to it with 1,000 men on each. In double rank
of 500 the longitudinal distance occupied would
be only 1,000 feet, and the whole mass would
be within a manageable space. The embarkation could have been performed in the same
manner as in the case of the obelisks. In the

H

disembarkation, however, it is probable that the pontoon was floated in time of flood quite near to the point required and a canal cut from there to the exact site. The colossi at that time stood on the edge of the desert; at present the soil rises to a height of 7 feet above the base, and they are annually surrounded by water. The huge colossus of Rameses II., whose remains lie a short distance away, is of about the same weight, and was probably handled in the same manner. The number of men here mentioned could have transported any statue or stone now existing in Egypt or elsewhere, or any that are mentioned in such hieroglyphic texts as I am aware of; and I think it may be safely assumed that from 1,000 to 1,200 tons marked the limit of the capacity of ancient engineers in this direction; the distance to which the stones were transported was not of importance mechanically or otherwise to an Egyptian despot. If it could be moved a foot, it could be moved the length of Egypt if he wished it. Time alone was required.

Ancient writers give accounts of objects of greater dimensions, but not in remote times. The most marvellous is the account given by Herodotus of a temple of Latona in the city of Buto, near one of the mouths of the Nile. This, he says, was made of one single stone,

FIG. XXI.   FIRST COLOSSAL IMAGE OF AMENHOTEP III.
AT THEBES.

FIG. XXII.   SECOND COLOSSAL IMAGE.

40 cubits or 70 feet square. Supposing that
the walls were 6 feet thick, it has been estimated to weigh 5,000 tons. Most writers have
assumed that it was brought from Assouan;
but Herodotus says nothing about its being
moved, and it is quite possible that it was a
boulder cut into shape on the spot, like the
huge 70 feet Jain image on the top of a hill at
Shravana Belagola in Mysore, and the still
more remarkable Kylas at Ellora in Hyder-
abad, a veritable cathedral, 365 feet long, 192
feet wide, and 96 feet high, cut out of the solid
rock, hollowed out and carved, both inside and
out with the most elaborate sculptures. Supposing that the 5,000 ton temple had been
dragged from Assouan, it would have required
75,000 men, and it is doubtful if even the Egyptians could have drilled so large a body of men
to the long pull, the strong pull, and the pull
all together that would have been necessary.
Moreover this was in the age of Psamthek,
B.C. 664, when Egypt had an open port at Naukratis, where there was a large Greek colony.
Latona was the mother of Apollo, and a temple
to her was undoubtedly owing to Greek in-
fluences. Herodotus also mentions a chapel
of a single stone that Amasis, B.C. 570, caused
to be brought from Assouan to Sais, but its
weight was only 480 tons, far less than the

colossi at Thebes.   It was brought by 2,000
men, ' all pilots," and three years were occupied in the transit.   This muster of men would
have been only one-third of the number required to drag it by main strength, and, as
Herodotus says, that the king would not allow
it to enter the sacred precincts, because one of
the men employed at the levers was crushed by
it, one might infer that they used capstans, for
injuries to men by capstan bars are not at all
uncommon on board ship.   Whether the Egyptians of the time of Psamthek and Amasis employed capstans or not the Assyrians, at about
the same date, used nothing of the sort, for the
sculptured slabs in the British Museum, discovered by Layard at Nineveh, show colossal
stone bulls in the time of Sennacherib, B.C. 704
to 676, drawn on sledges by men ; rollers are
placed under the sledges and huge levers are
used in rear.   Finally the sledge is drawn up
an inclined plain constructed of earth, and the
colossus is placed.   The Egyptians were probably no further advanced than this.   The
lifting and transporting of modern buildings
weighing tens of thousands of tons by means of
jacks far exceeds anything ever attempted by the
ancients.

The method of water transportation of obelisks by modern engineers is practically the

same as that of the ancient Egyptians, except that being obliged to take them over sea, the obelisks have been stowed in the hold instead of on deck. The Romans built huge vessels for the purpose, the one which carried the Vatican obelisk having 300 rowers and carrying a ballast of 120,000 modii,—1,000 tons,—of lentils, a small round grain, which was probably simply carried in sacks to fill in solidly round the obelisk and assist in preventing it from shifting when the vessel rolled. The Paris obelisk was carried from Luxor to Paris in a sailing lighter or barge, with a removable end, specially made at Toulon for the purpose. The London obelisk was carried in a specially made iron cylinder, which was towed by a steamer, and the New York obelisk was carried in an ordinary steamer bought for the purpose at Alexandria, a hole being cut in the bow, like the loading port of a timber ship, and the obelisk dragged into the fore hold. The land transportation was effected by the Romans and French in a chamulcus or cradle, which was pulled along greased ways by means of tackles and capstans. In the case of the English obelisk the iron cylinder, which was brought to Alexandria in pieces, was built round it just as it lay near the sea shore, wooden rings were built round this at the ends, and it was rolled

into the water as recommended by Paeonius at
the temple of Ephesus 2,500 years before.
Arrived in London it was brought directly to
the site on the Thames embankment, the
cylinder taken to pieces and the obelisk slid
sidewise on greased ways to the point of erection. The New York obelisk was transported
on land for several miles on iron balls, between
two iron channels, after the manner of Count
Carburi in moving the 600 ton pedestal of the
statue of Peter the Great from Karelia to St.
Petersburg; but trouble occurred to Gorringe
from the splitting of the channel irons, and
resort was had with success to the system of the
ordinary marine railway, where rollers are used
between metal ways. In one of the chambers
at Karnak are quantities of stone balls, which
some consider to have been used in this way by
the Egyptians, but they are all made of soft
stone, and are more likely to have been used
for catapults or cannon, and are probably not at
all ancient.

Colonel Wilks in the Transactions of the
Royal Society of Edinburgh in 1821, thus
describes the transportation of an obelisk made
and erected by natives at Seringapatam to the
memory of Dr. Webb in 1805. As the colonel's
remembrance of the exact dimensions was not
clear, I have obtained through the kindness

of Colonel J. Desaivylles, Chief Commandant
Mysore state troops, an exact drawing, fig. xxiii.,
which shows the dimensions to
be 3 × 3 × 52 feet.   This gives
a weight of about 35 tons, only
the tenth part of that of the
huge Egyptian obelisks ; but
the methods employed both for
transportation and erection are
so primitive that they might well
have been Egyptian.   The
stone having been detached
from the ledge [which was in a
quarry about two miles from the
site] with iron wedges in the
manner described in the chapter
on quarrying, the narrative pro-
ceeds as follows:—" The obelisk
was first blocked out in the
rough, to lighten it, before being
placed on its carriage, by means
which will easily be
conceived, after de-
scribing those used for
its erection.   The car-
riage, after repeatedly

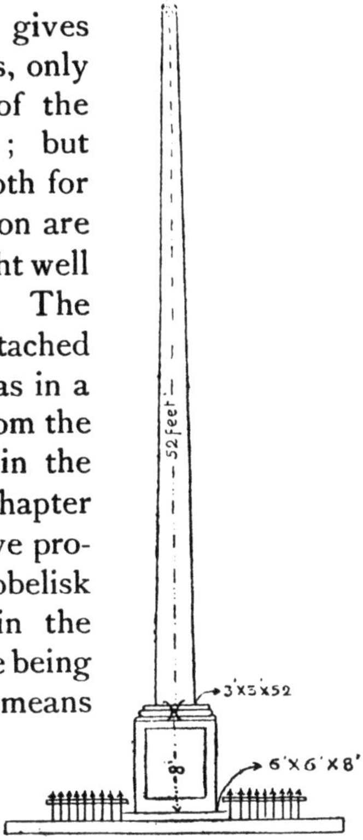

FIG. XXIII.   OBELISK AT
SERINGAPATAM, INDIA.

sinking into the hard road, as into a swamp,
was ultimately moved over a succession of
balks of timber, placed to support it.   Granite

is so excessively brittle, that it was thought hazardous to employ draught cattle or any power less manageable than that of men: and the number employed at one time, on the drag ropes, as well as I can venture to say, from the picture left on my memory, was about 600 men." The carriage was made of heavy timber. It had four inner and four outer wheels, and is not so practical as an Egyptian sledge, which according to my calculation would have required 525 men, and would have distributed the weight of the obelisk more evenly over the road bed. It is to be noted that the Indians preferred men to cattle on account of their superior intelligence.

CHAPTER VI.

THE ERECTION OF BUILDINGS AND MONUMENTS.

As has been shown, the knowledge which we possess concerning the ancient methods of transporting monuments is very limited; but with regard to their method of erecting them we have no knowledge whatever. In the building of temples Wilkinson thinks that a rude kind of crane was employed, and this seems probable. The side walls, where there was space, could easily have been built by the use of inclined planes; but the sectional columns of the halls and courts would present a difficulty in the matter of vertical alignment if surrounded by earth as they ascended, whereas a scaffolding of poles lashed together by ropes, such as the Japanese build, would easily support a single pulley crane for hoisting the disks or quadrants of which the columns are composed. The walls of Deir el Bahri would doubtless have given us full information regarding the erection of obelisks, but unfortunately the Coptic Christians destroyed it, and it only remains to describe in general terms the methods adopted by modern

engineers in handling the same objects, and try
to deduce from these the most probable course

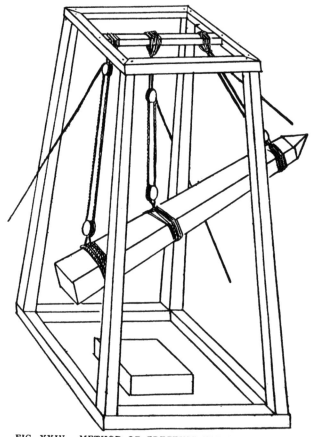

FIG. XXIV.   METHOD OF ERECTING VATICAN OBELISK.

followed by the Egyptians themselves.   The
Romans, so far as we know from the curious

account by Ammianus Marcellinus, of the original erection of the Lateran obelisk by the Emperor Constantine, A.D. 345, always erected a high framework over the pedestal and lifted the obelisk bodily from the ground by means of tackles, lowering it upon brass blocks placed upon the pedestal. These blocks were usually of the form of crabs because the obelisk in one sense symbolized a ray of the sun, and the crab belonged to Apollo the sun god. The Egyptians always rested their obelisks with the base flat upon the pedestal, and it is therefore probable that they never lifted them bodily. In either case an obelisk is much more firm than its appearance would indicate. Taking the average of those now standing at Luxor, Paris, London, and New York, it would require about 25 tons pressure at the top to push one over, or about 75 tons if applied to the whole side as in the case of a wind. A hurricane would not exert more than a quarter of this amount of pressure. Fig. xxiv. represents Fontana's method in 1580, which was similar to that of the Romans. He erected a huge structure, composed of beams a metre square, which was nicknamed " Fontana's Castle," and by means of tackles, capstans, and levers, he lifted and lowered the obelisk and transported it to the Vatican where the castle was re-erected and the operation reversed. An excellent painting of it can be seen in the Vatican. The Egyptians probably had no knowledge of multiplying power by the use of tackles, and without such knowledge this method would have been impossible to them.   No number of single fixed pulleys would have sufficed.   Next in chronological order is the monument of Dr. Webb at Seringapatam, in 1805, which is thus

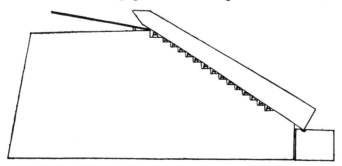

FIG. XXV.   METHOD OF ERECTING SERINGAPATAM OBELISK.
ELEVATION.

described by Colonel Wilks (figs. xxv. xxvi.) :
" Conceive the shaft finished, and placed ready for erection, in a horizontal position raised to the proper height, and with its base accurately placed for insertion in the top of the pedestal, when it should attain a vertical position.   Then imagine a strong wall, built at right angles with the line of the shaft, and a few feet beyond its smaller end: with two lateral retaining walls parallel to the shaft, and a fourth, of smaller

elevation, near the pedestal, to support the mass of earth, and the workmen to be employed. On such a platform raised 10½ feet, you will, in the first instance, conceive the shaft to be horizontally arranged. Two lines of timber, plank, or balk, were then ranged along the two sides of the shaft, to serve as fulcra, and two lines of

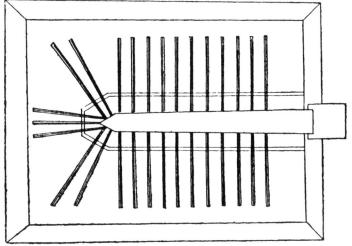

FIG. XXVI. METHOD OF ERECTING SERINGAPATAM OBELISK.
PLAN.

men, with handspikes, attended by others with chocks, or pieces of timber, of different thickness, to be inserted under the shaft, for the purpose of keeping the elevation of the smaller end, effected by the handspikes, and distributing the pressure so equally, as not to risk the accidents which would otherwise be inevitable, with this

very fragile substance. In proportion as elevation was thus gradually obtained for the smaller
end, the space below was filled with rammed
earth, and the same process was repeated, with
the parallel balks of timber, handspikes and
chocks; the small end gradually rising at each
successive step, the wall behind increasing in
height and an inclined plane of solid earth
gradually increasing its angle with the horizon,
until it equalled that at which solid earth could
with safety be employed, when the force required
being proportionately diminished, timber alone
was employed for its elevation. Finally a
scaffolding of timber was erected embracing
three sides of the pedestal, and nearly equal to
the ultimate height of the obelisk : ropes were
applied to the summit of the shaft, in such di-
rections as to steady and check it : handspikes
gave the requisite impetus until it felt the power
of the ropes, and was ultimately and safely
lodged in its shallow receptacle." Here is a
method which is absolutely primitive, and it is
well within the bounds of reasonable conjecture
that it was derived from the Egyptians themselves. It is a method that is perfectly safe
and is practical whether it is applied to an
obelisk of 35 tons or 350 tons. The only limi-
tation is the horizontal space required, for it is
obvious that the heavier the obelisk the more

extensive must be the gradually rising platform inclosing the inclined plane, in order to afford room for levers of the necessary length.

The French method (1832) is next in order. It is shown in fig. xxvii.   Its simplicity is such that it requires but little explanation.   A wide, high frame derrick is placed nearly at right angles to the obelisk, and a heavy lashing is passed from the top of this frame round the head of the obelisk.   Tackles being also attached to the top of this frame, they are hauled upon

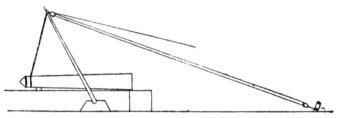

FIG. XXVII.   METHOD OF ERECTING PARIS OBELISK.

until the obelisk is vertical, the derrick pivoting upon its heel while the obelisk pivots upon the edge of its base.   The reverse operation was pursued in lowering the obelisk at Luxor.   The instinctive idea of anyone looking at an obelisk is that it was raised by lifting the head while the base rested on the pedestal, and the second thought is that the edge would be splintered in the effort unless provision was made for it. Nearly all the obelisks that we see out of Egypt are more or less splintered at the bottom. They have all been moved more than once, and the base has probably suffered in consequence. Le Bas' method of protecting the base was ingenious; he cut away the edge of the pedestal underneath the Luxor obelisk, and inserted a long, square oak block having a semicircular groove in the upper part lying just underneath the edge of the base of the obelisk, and fitted to this edge a long, round oak block which corresponded exactly with the semicircular groove in the pedestal block. He thus had a hinge which functioned perfectly when he lowered the obelisk. Le Bas says that in the pedestal of the obelisk remaining at Luxor there is a semicircular groove just underneath the edge of the obelisk, and he thinks that the ancient Egyptians utilized it for a hinge; but he does not say if there was one in the pedestal of the obelisk which he removed, and there is none visible in the pedestal of Hatasoo's obelisks at Karnak. The principles involved in Le Bas' method are such as the Egyptians must have been well acquainted with, the only difference being that Le Bas used manifold tackles and capstans and employed a dozen Europeans and a hundred or two of Arabs, whereas the Egyptians would have used either single pulleys or none at all, and would have employed huge ropes and thousands of men. The method would have been applicable either alone or in conjunction with a partial application of the Indian method where there was no room for the latter alone, as in the case of Queen Hatasoo's obelisks, which were erected in a narrow court or hall where there was, according to Wilkinson, no space for inclined planes and levers, and where, according to Budge, one side of the hall was already occupied by pillars.

The London obelisk (fig. xxviii.), was first brought to a horizontal position over the pedestal and then raised bodily in that position by means of blocking and hydraulic jacks. When about half its ultimate height a pair of metal trunnions were strapped to its centre of gravity and a frame with movable girders placed under the trunnions ; the blocking was then removed and the obelisk swung to the vertical position and lowered to the pedestal. The New York obelisk was handled by the same system of trunnions, both for lowering it at Alexandria and for re-erecting it at New York ; but it is not probable that the ancient Egyptians could have utilized this method, as it could not have been adopted at all with any other material than iron and steel, and in these they were lacking.

Many curious theories have been advanced

I

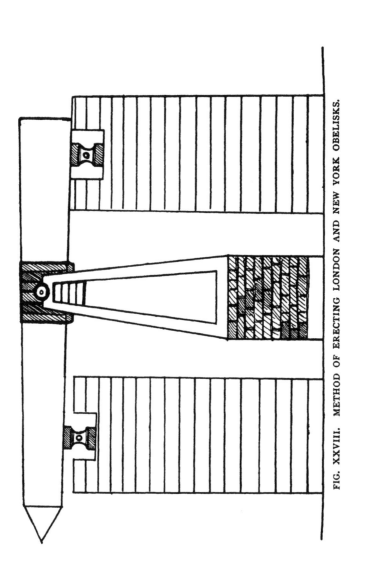

FIG. XXVIII. METHOD OF ERECTING LONDON AND NEW YORK OBELISKS.

from time to time to account for the erection of Egyptian obelisks : but none of them are practical. Sharpe thinks it was by inclined planes, and Cooper by rollers of continually increasing diameter, as though inclined planes and rollers were animated objects. Another writer suggests surrounding the obelisk with a tank of water, and attaching a float to the upper end, without thinking how large would be the tank required and how impossible of erection at any of the localities where obelisks were used, and a still later writer, in 1898, thinks that an obelisk could be dragged up an inclined plane base first and then allowed to slide down a steep incline on the other side to its pedestal, without suggesting any method of disposing of the force that would drag it up or any method of controlling it, a far more serious matter, when it was sliding down.

It seems probable that in most cases the Indian method and the French method were used in conjunction, in such a manner that ropes were led from the head of the obelisk over some high object erected in the vicinity, or led horizontally from a vertical frame astride of the obelisk. By attaching a large number of men to these ropes, the work of the men at the levers under the head of the obelisk would be materially assisted. Whether the pylon of the temple

could be utilized is doubtful on account of the
lack of space behind it for handling the men :
but there would be no lack of space parallel to
the pylon. Take, for example, a specific case,
that of the remaining Luxor obelisk. If M. Le
Bas was right in his interpretation of the groove
in its pedestal, this obelisk was brought from
the river in a direction parallel to the pylon of
the temple, and placed with its base over the
hinge groove and the hinge attached, or the
edge itself might possibly have been allowed to
travel in the groove or to rest on the surface,
protected by some tough substance like raw
hide : a stout heel lashing was then passed
round the upper edge of the base of the obelisk
and secured to stakes driven into the ground.
This would prevent the obelisk from slipping
when the head commenced to rise. If the
Egyptians did not have the wit to build a frame
derrick astride the obelisk, as M. Le Bas did,
then they must have built a wall on the other
side of the pedestal at right angles to the pylon,
and nearly as high as the obelisk would be when
erected. The ropes were then led over the top
of this wall. With the derrick, M. le Bas found
that a pull of 113 tons was sufficient to raise his
obelisk, which weighed 225 tons, without the
use of levers under its head. This would cor-
respond to about 8,000 men. With the wall

one would be obliged to add about 50 per cent.,
increasing the number to 12,000 men, on account
of the bad lead and the friction ; but the power
required would diminish very rapidly as the
obelisk commenced to rise.   Such a force could
be handled within a space of about 1,000 feet
long and 48 wide, which would be about the
length of the inclined plane on the other side
of the wall, by means of which it was built.
The obelisk could be raised from the horizontal
to the vertical in a few moments ; but as the
obelisks were precious objects, and such crude
machinery, and great numbers of men difficult
to control, it seems reasonable that the obelisk
would be raised by small increments, and filled
in underneath with bags of sand or mud bricks
at each rise, so that there should be no danger
at any time.   Everything being arranged before-
hand, it would be a matter of a few days at most
to put the obelisk in place.   In the case of
Queen Hatasoo's obelisks, it is impossible to
judge of the former conditions from the present
state of the ruins.   It is to be presumed, however, that the end walls of the temple would
have been partially removed, if necessary, to
obtain a lead for the ropes, and an inclined
plane filling the entire breadth of the hall could
have been built as the obelisk rose, which would
have afforded room for men with levers on one
side of it.

I 2

Regarding the Egyptian method of transporting and erecting standing statues we are no
wiser than in regard to obelisks. They were
probably transported horizontally and raised in
the same manner as obelisks, where there was
space for it; but there are some still remaining
in positions which point directly to the use of
the jack for their final adjustment at least. An
interesting example of how much power is required to handle one of these huge masses is
afforded by Major Bagnold's experiences in 1887
in lifting out of the mud the two statues of
Rameses the Great, so familiar to Egyptian
travellers at Memphis. One is of limestone,
and weighs about 100 tons (fig. xxix.) the other
of granite, weighing about 60 tons. The
former was found in a pool with a small portion
of the back exposed, and the latter about 200
yards away, with its left shoulder and crown
projecting from the mud. The operation was
successfully accomplished in three months and
a half, and the statues placed in their present
horizontal positions beyond the reach of high
Nile. In the Appendix is given a list of what
Major Bagnold thinks are essential for a work
of this kind. The list is taken from the Pro-
ceedings of the Society of Biblical Archæology
of June 5th, 1888, and is of very great interest
when one remembers that the ancient Egypt-

FIG. XXIX.   COLOSSUS OF RAMESES THE GREAT, AT MEMPHIS.
Society of Biblical Archæology.

ians not only brought these statues hundreds of miles by land and water, but they erected them, and yet no monument, no tomb, and no temple shows the method by which they were erected, and this, too, in a land whose people were so fond of pictorial representation, that there is no act in life, no occupation, no profession, no recreation, no trade, and no art that is not fully painted on the walls of their wonderful tombs. Was it because these methods were not considered noteworthy, or was it because the priests forbid it?

We in Europe and America are very proud of our wonderful mechanical achievements, of our bridges, tunnels, towers, and churches, and the indomitable daring and energy of our engineers; but other lands and other climes have seen their wonders as well, and the monuments of the past have still their lessons to teach. The giant ruins of the Mingoon Pagoda, the exquisite symmetry of the Taj-Mahal, the monumental labour of the Jewel Temple on Mount Abu, and the terraced magnificence of Borobodor, that Javan rival to the pyramid, all are instructive, for it was a daring architect who could contemplate and execute the least of them. We moderns are confident, but what modern could compare in sublime audacity with Dimocrates of Macedon, who proposed to

Alexander that "he should carve Mount Athos into the statue of a man with a city in one hand, and a basin in the other, which should receive all the waters of the mountain and again discharge them into the sea."

APPENDIX.

List of Camp Equipment, Tools, Appliances, and Materials employed in raising the two Colossi at Memphis.

ARTICLES.

Camp Equipment.

	No.
Bedsteads (portable), bedding, camp kettles, chairs, tables, &c., for 4 Europeans.	
Tents, Indian pattern, Double-Pole (Cotton)	1

Tools.

Carpenters' tools, complete in chest	sets	1
Masons' tools, complete, in chest	sets	1
Axes, pick		10
Bars, boring, $1\frac{1}{2}'' \times 6'$		2
„ crow, 5'		2
Bars, crow, 4'		2
Hammers, sledge		6
Mauls, wood, iron-hooped		10
Stones, grind		1
Tape, measuring...		1
Vices, standing, 36 lbs.		1

Appliances.

Barrows, wheel	12

Blocks, "Bothway's," 8" single 1

,, ,, ,, snatch 1

,, ,, ,, double 2

,, ,, ,, treble 2

,, malleable iron, 4" double 2

,, ,, ,, 5" snatch 2

Buckets, iron, galvanized 4

Cans, water (for filling jacks) 2

Carts, Maltese 1

,, tip 2

Cordage :—

  Hemp, tarred, 6" ... ... fathoms 20

  ,, ,, 3" ... ... ,, ... 250

  ,, ,, $1\frac{1}{2}$" ... ... ,, ... 113

  ,, white Manilla 2" ... ... ,, ... 120

  Hemp, spunyarn, 3-thread lbs. 10

  Steel, flexible, $1\frac{1}{2}$" ... ... fathoms 113

Capstans, "crab," frames, etc. 2

  ,, ,, bars 4

Chain-cable, $\frac{3}{4}$" ... ... fathoms 4

Drums or reels, for wire rope 1

Dogs, iron, sawyers', 12" 40

Gauges, pressure, hydraulic (to indicate to 3 tons per inch) 1

Hose-pipe, india rubber, $\frac{1}{4}$ in. ... ... yards 10

Jacks, hydraulic (Tangye's) 30-ton 2

  ,, ,, (Tannett and Walker's), 40-ton ... 4

  ,, ,, (Tangye's) 100-ton 2

Ladders, light, 15 ft., in 2 pieces 2

Pumps, "Bastier," chain, $2\frac{1}{2}$ in. with horse gear, to lift 20 ft. 1

Rails, iron, double-headed, with chairs 12

Rammers, iron-headed 6

Rollers, oak 3' 6" × 6" 60

Materials.

Cotton waste			50
Cement, Portland		...barrels as required.	
Grease, cart or wagon		cwts.	2
India rubber sheet, $\frac{1}{4}''$ thick		lbs.	10
Iron, galvanized, corrugated, ...		sheets	30
Lead, red		lbs.	4
Lime		cwts. as required.	
Nails, iron, spike 8 in.		lbs.	10
,, ,, ,, 10 in.		,,	20
,, ,, cut, 2 in.		,,	10
Oil, Rangoon		...gallons	2
,, sweet		,,	6
,, kerosine		,,	6
Screws, for wood, $1\frac{1}{2}$ in.		doz.	6
Tallow, Russian...		lbs.	100
Timber, fir :—			
Blocks, $2'\ 0'' \times 12'' \times 12''$			200
Baulks, $20' \times 12'' \times 12''$			2
,, $8' \times 10'' \times 10''$			4
Plank, $9'' \times \frac{1}{2}''$ ... ...ft. run.			150
*Sleepers, $7' \times 10'' \times 7''$			300
Timber, oak :—			
Pieces, $5'\ 0'' \times 11'' \times 5''$			6
Wire, steel, galvanized, 3-strand, 18 S.W.G. ...		cwt.	1

The above list is intended as a rough guide for any person who may set out to raise or move some heavy monument.

* Wedges were made from these as required : one sleeper being cut into four wedges.

www.ingramcontent.com/pod-product-compliance
Ingram Content Group UK Ltd.
Pitfield, Milton Keynes, MK11 3LW, UK
UKHW020349010325
455677UK00021B/367